D1343440

Please return on or before the date below.

Non-loan returns

Clifton Library √19
Rotherham College of Arts & Technology,
Eastwood Lane, Rotherham, S65 1EG
Need to renew, book a PC or book a help session?
Call: (01709) 722869 or 722738

ISBN:0692477896
ISBN-13: 978-0692477892

DEDICATION

Throughout most of my career I've had to make my own opportunities happen. My first writings for *Dancer* came about by my offer to editor Owen Goldman to supply a monthly column on jazz dance, for free, just because the paper had columns on ballet and tap dance but not on jazz dance. But there are many who have helped me along the way with their kindness, knowledge, and mentorship. For those reasons I'd like to thank Rosemary Boross for her introduction to dance and her decades of personal friendship; my stellar teachers of jazz dance - Nat Horne, Michael Owens, Frank Hatchett, and Billy Siegenfeld; my theatre dance and tap dance teachers Lee Theodore, Christopher Chadman, Paul Draper, and Bob Audy; my mentor at UC Irvine Donald McKayle; and most importantly my decades of work with the freestyle jazz dance legend Matt Mattox - your freestyle dance technique and style have given me a stellar blueprint for my life's work.

CONTENTS

Comments on Jazz Dance 1996-2014

ACKNOWLEDGMENTS

It's 2015, and I now mark my fortieth year as a jazz dancer. Whether as a performer or teacher, choreographer or author - jazz dance is a topic that has always been on my mind. My breadth of involvement reflects an obvious deeply felt affinity for this personal form of dance movement. I've always considered my jazz dance writing to be of less personal interest than my choreography, but assembling this book and realizing the volume and depth of my authorship has given me a new appreciation of my past literary efforts. When including my NYU master's degree thesis on the freestyle jazz dancer Matt Mattox, my research can be considered quite valuable to the serious student of jazz dance.

One aspect of my work that I am most proud of is giving voice to teachers and choreographers from jazz dance companies and musical theatre. For this reason my writings started with a jazz dance column in *Dancer* newspaper, with the desire to give visibility to those jazz dancers who were not considered as worthy of mention in scholarly journals. Eventually I decided to focus more on my own choreographic work and less on writing about others. But my choreography has benefited from knowledge gained from writing and written research, making it all a worthwhile endeavor.

My thanks to my many publishers who have given permission to reprint my articles - *Dancer, Dance Teacher, Dance Magazine, Dance Chronicle, JazzPulsions,* and the University Press of Florida.

Most of all I'd like to acknowledge the rich history of jazz music and jazz dance. The joys of its expression have inspired me throughout all of my adult life. It has burned bright in my soul from the moment it touched me...and it still continues to give me a compelling reason to get up each and every day and experience its passion, conviction, and joy.

ABOUT THE AUTHOR

Bob Boross is known internationally for his artistic excellence in jazz, tap, and musical theatre dance. Bob's career began as a musical theatre performer in productions of *West Side Story*, *Godspell*, *Zorba*, and *The Pirates of Penzance* (Pirate King). He made his Broadway debut in the 1981 revival of *Can-Can*, choreographed by Roland Petit. Since then he has choreographed Equity and non-Equity productions of *Annie Get Your Gun*, *Guys and Dolls*, *Victor/Victoria*, *Blood Brothers*, *A Funny Thing Happened on the Way to the Forum*, and *The Best Little Whorehouse in Texas*. Bob has also been invited to teach and choreograph by jazz dance companies in Sweden, Russia, France, England, Finland, Italy, and Mexico. Most recently his work has been seen on multiple occasions in the *NY Jazz Choreography Project* and the *Choreographer's Canvas* (NYC) and *VelocityDC Dance Festival* in Washington DC. In Los Angeles Bob has presented his work in *Jazz Dance LA* at the Japanese-American Theatre, *Spectrum Dance in LA* at the Ivar Theatre in Hollywood, and at the *Gypsy Dance Awards* show at the Beverly Hilton Hotel. His evening length dance theatre piece *Empty Sky...The Rising*, set to twelve songs by Bruce Springsteen, debuted in 2005 at the Two River Theatre in NJ.

Bob's dance approach is mainly influenced by the jazz dance pioneer Matt Mattox and his freestyle jazz dance technique. Over the years Bob's students have enjoyed great success - dancing on Broadway, in films, music videos, ballet companies, in Las Vegas, on the Academy Awards, and as finalists in the shows *So You Think You Can Dance* and *Step Up and Dance* (Bravo network).

Bob holds the M.A. in Individualized Study (Jazz Dance) from the Gallatin School of New York University and a B.A. in Economics from

Denison University. He has held professorships at Illinois State University, Western Kentucky University, and the University of California, Irvine, where he was appointed head of jazz dance. At Stephens College in Missouri, Bob served as Associate Professor and Chairperson of the dance department. In Virginia, Bob has taught at Radford University and as Visiting Associate Professor of Jazz Dance at Shenandoah Conservatory. Bob is also known as an author on jazz dance, and his writings have been published in *Dance Chronicle*, *Dance Magazine*, *Dance Teacher*, and *Dancer*. Since 2003 he has been an invited member of the Advisory Board of *Dance Teacher* magazine.

For more information, visit www.bobboross.com.

Photo credits:

Cover photos - dance image - Univ of California, Irvine

promotional image; Dancers – Jessica Summers and Spencer

Smith, photo – Frank Peters. From *Love Fell Out With Me* –

choreography by Bob Boross. Headshot – by Mike Quain.

Back cover photo – Cathryn Lynne

Photos in *Empty Sky...The Rising*; A Response to Catastrophe

through Dance - Eduardo Patino.

Photos in articles on Matt Mattox, Billy Siegenfeld, and Donald

McKayle – by Bob Boross.

Un-credited photos have been supplied by interviewees.

2

1
JEANNIE HILL –
HOW DO YOU TEACH JAZZ DANCE?

Reprinted from *Dancer* with permission, Copyright June 1996

Nat Horne, the noted teacher of jazz dance, begins his classes with the declaration "Jazz is a feeling!" It's not the latest step on a video, or the standard competition choreographic pattern of switch splits and double turn-split-down to the floor. At its core, jazz is the joyous feeling of release that radiates outward from a person's soul. It is personal expression, and although a group of people may hear and react to the same jazz song, their movements most likely will be individual and unique. This quality of personal identification is what makes jazz special, and is exactly the thing that is lacking in so much of what we today call "jazz dance." Music and lifestyles in today's society really don't encourage individuality. The teaching of jazz dance has been overwhelmed by the straight beat of pop music, and the total dependence on repetition to achieve a technically proficient body instrument. The result is that we have a dance population that looks good doing movement that they have envisioned is jazz dance, but really is ignorant of the inner spark that lights the jazz flame in the soul. We assume poses, but we aren't connected, we don't "feel." Don't believe it? Just ask a group of young dancers to "move to the music" - improvise. Most likely you will see a rehash of classroom steps, or a nonplussed dancer who sheepishly grins and nervously stands still - like a fish out of water. They plead "Tell me what to do!"

Luckily, there are dancers, teachers, and choreographers working today who are connected to the feeling of jazz, and are using that as the basis of their artistic expression. One such choreographer is Jeannie Hill. If you have attended any of Gus Giordano's Jazz Dance Congresses, no doubt you were impressed by the Jump Rhythm Jazz Project, composed of Jeannie and founder Billy Siegenfeld. This bubbly duo has interpreted the classic strains of jazz composers like Ellington, Basie, Parker, and others in concert dances that explore the physical embodiment of jazz music, as well as excite and entertain their audience. Illinois State University was fortunate in recently having Jeannie Hill as a guest artist, teaching classes in classic jazz dance and choreographing the concert piece *Ya Dig?*

So how does Hill educate her dancers about jazz dance? How does she start the process of getting them to look inside themselves for feeling, rather than assuming feeling? Her first method is to use jazz music. Real jazz music. Music that swings, with sections of improvisation. Then, rather than starting her class facing the mirror and delivering a series of commands for the dancers to execute, she simply has them "walk." Anywhere in the room, in any direction - but

just walk in time to the jazz beat. Get used to this new feeling of rebound in the swing jazz beat that you may never have felt before. And look at the other people as you pass them. Smile, laugh, play off of each other - react. Physically say whatever the music makes you feel at the moment. Some dancers quickly pick up and free themselves to interact, while others are hindered by their self consciousness. Hill's next device is to divide the measure into four beats, and then have the dancers hit a pose on either the first, second, third, or fourth beat. No particular pose, just do whatever you feel at that moment. Let the music fill you, feel it, and react. This is done first in the walking pattern, and then with all dancers in a tight circle facing inward. By this time the dancers are laughing and actually enjoying making up new physical accents on the spot. Personalities are starting to emerge, with some dancers making up angular dance poses, while others opt for comical exaggerations. Then dancers begin to simultaneously notice unique accents by others, and find joy in reacting and urging each other on. Individuality is encouraged.

4

Her class then progresses into some more traditional technique exercises (*pliés, tendus,* extensions, etc), but always tempered by the swing beat of jazz music. And the exercises are executed not in 1-2-3-4 counts, but with syncopated accents that encourage the dancer to display rhythmic awareness as well as technique. The dancer must soak up the jazz beat, and let the technical exercises flow from a body that derives its impulse to move first from feeling and understanding of rhythm. In this way, the dancer enjoys the music and the connection to what Hill calls the "joy factor." The dancer responds by taking charge of the exercise more so than in standard classes where dancers merely repeat de facto movements.

In Hill's class, the dancer finds the personal connection to the movement, instilled by the dancer's tapping into their own feelings and reactions, that drives the technique exercise and gives it a new sense of purpose. The movement is self motivated, with the result that each dancer may execute the technique exercise slightly different. One person may hit a musical accent by adding a tiny side contraction. Another may lift a shoulder and close one eye. Why? Because that's how the music makes her feel at that moment. Now, if there are problems with dancers executing movements in a technical fashion, Hill will stop and make the proper correction. But the important factor is the allowance for and encouragement of individuality of expression. And feeling the music. Even in basic technique exercises, she has allowed for and encouraged the use of improvisation so that the dancers can add something of their own, developing personal style and the ability to feel and react. And one occurrence is apparent - throughout all of the exercises, everyone is smiling. They are experiencing the "joy factor," becoming sensitive to what jazz is all about while bettering their technique.

Hill synthesizes the rhythmic and technical aspects of her class with a final combination. She draws from everyday movements like walking and running as well as "dance" movements like double turns and *developpes*. But what is most apparent is her use of the body as a rhythmic percussion instrument. The rhythms of the music are reflected and physicalized within her body as razor sharp whips of the arms, popping shoulders, and flick kicks that crackle with intensity. Her feet patter and skip across the floor as she lays down the rhythm not with counts but by scat singing the accents and then requesting that the dancers do the same. Or her movements may become syrupy smooth, oozing through a sixteen count layout that commands the viewer's attention by matching the timing of the anticipated ending with the end of the musical phrase. She transmits the tension inherent at the final moment of imbalance at the conclusion of the layout to the audience by contrasting the smooth physical dynamic against the bopping musical accompaniment. Always, the feeling of jazz music drives the movements, which are developed through a process of improvisation. And flourishes of individual style within the movement are encouraged through the dancer's own sense of improvisation and feeling. The class ends on a note of exuberance and exhilaration that one feels after experiencing a truly special event.

Jeannie Hill's movement embodies many of the defining factors of jazz - improvisation, individuality, spontaneity, and rhythm. And her class is designed specifically to address and develop those qualities in her students. It is an approach, unlike so much of today's classes, that rightly deserves to be called "jazz dance." And it is an approach that carries over into the choreographic world of concert jazz dance. In next month's column, I will examine more of Hill's philosophy of jazz dance and how she created the concert piece *Ya Dig?* for the Illinois State Dance Theatre.

2
JEANNIE HILL –
ANATOMY OF A JAZZ DANCE

Reprinted from *Dancer* with permission, Copyright July 1996

Jazz dance allows for and encourages personal expression, making the possibilities inherent in jazz dance expression as varied as the human imagination. Jazz is about feeling and improvisation. When a jazz dancer improvises, he or she is expressing that person's unique reaction to a phrase of jazz music, or even just an imagined rhythmic groove. Now, the question is, "Is this jazz improvisation an art form?" Is merely watching another person's improvisation an artistic event? In some cases, yes. Any display of Gregory Hines and his "improvography" is artistic, as are the characterizations of jazz dancer James Berry (of the Berry Brothers). But it can also be said that much improvisation is self centered and meanders like a creek that wanders and disappears into the distance - it exists, but where is it going?

These examples represent individual expressions. But what about group dances? Can a group of people improvise independently of each other and still create a concert dance? In my view, probably not. A dance of this sort needs a structure and a reason for being that has to be determined by a conceptualist - the choreographer. That is the person who sets the parameters for choices of movement, music, costumes, lights, etc, in order to coordinate the efforts of all dancers in a pre-determined direction. When this direction, or theme, is realized, the audience then absorbs and is affected by the impact of the dance, and that is what makes it artistic. This may involve the use of improvisation to set movement, or by certain dancers at certain times within the piece for a specific reason, but usually never without parameters.

This pattern of improvisation and jazz feeling was used by choreographer Jeannie Hill when she staged *Ya Dig?* for the Illinois State Dance Theatre. Hill, as a member of Manhattan Tap and the Jump Rhythm Jazz Project, is known for creating dances that are true to the jazz philosophy of exploration of rhythm and experiencing what she calls the "joy factor." This is the moment when a dancer reacts to the release of jazz music by finding a corresponding release in the dancer's physical and mental state. Its when the body sings like a jazz "groove." Finding this groove is the ultimate for all jazz musicians, and something that only the hippest musicians can attain. It is like a mystical state of oneness with the jazz feeling. This attainment and respect for the joy factor is the basis of her piece *Ya Dig?*

Hill starts with the music, and then uses it to spur her movement choices. In this case, it was "Filthy McNasty" by Horace Silver and sung by Dee Dee Bridgewater. (As she often says with a wink, "Only the best musicians in my class!"). This song is about a legendary musician named Filthy McNasty who is so good and hits the groove so hard that others say he is "bad." He is so bad, he's dirty - filthy dirty! Only the hippest can appreciate the stellar level of Filthy's groove, so she centered the piece around eight dancers who first eye each other warily, evaluating their rivals for their "hipness" and ability to truly appreciate Filthy's stratospheric jamming. As it progresses the characters, dressed in loose black pants and tight shirts with rolled up sleeves, break into a group of five and then a trio as they dig on the groove in their own way. Slowly, they realize that they are all OK, that everyone is hip to Filthy, and the place blows out into a jam session. It becomes a physicalization of the music, with trios and duos blasting out the rhythms of the music with rhythmic accents in the body. Some dancers burst into vernacular steps like jitterbug kicks, while others contrast the musical mayhem with legato phrases of movement. A centerpiece is a section with two trios and a duo, each knocking out rhythms that are inspired by different instruments in the band. At its conclusion, after everyone has had his or her turn to cut loose, they slowly wind down and offer conciliatory glances, acknowledging that "Yeah, we came, we saw, we grooved!" It ends with the dancers in a tight circle, arms slowly billowing from the center as the music crescendos, and a symbolic unison leap to the heavens as the lights black out, leaving the dancers suspended in mid-air in an incarnate picture of the joy factor.

I had a chance to speak with Jeannie Hill about her process in creating a jazz dance. For her, the music is her starting point and her inspiration. In this piece she is taking the concept of the music, lyrics, and scat singing, and using that to set her scene. It determines the characterizations of the dancers, and gives them a motivation. The tension of the initial wariness is important in helping her to choose specific movements, as is the release of that tension when the dancers relent and accept each other. By assigning a setting and a reason why the dancers are within that setting, she has given a cohesiveness to all of the actions of the dance. The dance now has a purpose, or a theme.

As for developing specific movement, Hill relies on the jazz basic of improvisation. She listens to the music, identifies a rhythm or groove she likes, and then dances by herself until she finds a phrase that she feels represents what the music says and what each character would be feeling. At other times, rather than imitating the rhythm of the music, she composes her own rhythm and applies it as a counterpoint to the music. In this way she is like a jazz musician improvising a solo over an established beat. As for vernacular steps, Hill says that jazz music is of the people, like folk dance, and that steps from social dances like the lindy or jitterbug are viable sources for movement to jazz music. It is the kind of movement any average person would respond with when dancing to swinging jazz.

Hill has allowed each dancer, through personal improvisation, the opportunity to add individual touches to established patterns of movement. In the instances of solos, she has worked with the unique talents of the dancer to create movement specifically suited to their abilities and personalities. She has also made conscious choices as to costumes and lighting so that the edge of the dancers is further heightened. Her role of artistic choreographer - a conceptualist who mixes the ingredients of theme, music, movement, costumes, lighting, title, etc. - is validated by the success of the piece. Her identity as a jazz dance artist is visible in her use of rhythm, improvisation, accent, dynamics, and outwardly radiating movements and energy. And the directed, conditional use of improvisation as opposed to the meandering stream model has enabled her to create fresh, and most importantly, purposeful movement.

The culmination of this concerted group effort is the evocation of the "joy factor." The audience can't help but be caught up in the waves of energy that radiate from the dancers as they demonstrate what makes Filthy the revered musician he is. The sharing of the joy with the audience, in my estimation, is what makes this piece an artistic dance. By allowing the audience to experience the joy and the groove, they are let in on the secret of jazz and thereby enlightened as to where that place resides within.

Ya dig?

3
REFLECTIONS ON THE 1996
WORLD JAZZ DANCE CONGRESS

Reprinted from *Dancer* with permission, Copyright September 1996

The spectrum of life experience has been expressed in the medium of jazz. Pain and sorrow, smooth grooves, comical characterizations, and ultimate exhilaration stream forth from the sounds of jazz music, and over the years dancers have responded by physicalizing those emotions in jazz dance. Jazz can say it all - and that is what troubled me about the 1996 Jazz Dance World Congress. This monumental gathering of dancers, teachers, and companies from around the globe was long on the commercial aspects of jazz dance, and short on its artistic expression. There was plenty of sizzle, but for this observer, not enough steak.

Unfortunately, due to teaching schedules, I was only able to observe three days of classes and two nights of performances out of the five day Congress. My thoughts are based on what I witnessed during that time. Hopefully more was presented to dispel my notions, and if it was, I'm sure that you will let me know.

On the plus side, its is certainly obvious that jazz dancers know how to entertain. There was no shortage of talented dancers and choreographers who could mesmerize an audience with deft displays of choreographic pyrotechnics. Especially noteworthy is the state of technical training being given to our young dancers. While observing classes and performances, I saw numerous teenage dancers capable of tossing off multiple turns that effortlessly descended to floor slides and splits in remarkably imaginative ways. In a class taught by Joe Tremaine, line after line of young dancers flawlessly executed a very fast *chaine/* double stepover turn combination across the carpeted Kennedy Center lobby floor. Our future dancers know how to get your attention.

But then, how do we keep that attention? It seems that jazz dancers, or at least the demographics of this gathering, are getting too comfortable with the three minute time limit basic to all dance competitions. In that format, you have just a moment to make an impression, so the tendency is to forgo any development of concept or story and just give the judges what you've got. An electrifying turn combo or a slowly ascending *developpe* gets the technical points from the judges and the whoops and hollers from the audience but Joe Q. Dancegoer, as when having a second or third bowl of ice cream, gets a bit weary of being force fed second position splits ad finitum. Its OK for Mom and Dad and the rest of the dancer's cheering squad, but the sophisticated dance fan tends to look at dance on a deeper level.

And this is why I am troubled. About jazz dance, and its continued growth and acceptance. Jazz dance is being limited by the financial pressures of making a living in today's world. The media has become an overwhelming influence on today's youth, and is presenting a narrow scope of musical and movement choices. Kids today see only the current culture, and bring the desire to experience that culture into the dance studios. As a former studio owner myself, I can't tell you how many phone calls I received from parents of children who wanted to learn a dance from a specific video. This aggregate demand translates into dollars - money to be spent - and studio owners feel the need to comply or perish.

Then, as one aspect of jazz dance becomes dominant, conventions capitalize on its popularity and present one style predominantly. Our dancers are going through their dance careers with blinders on, ignorant of the rich heritage of social and theatrical dance styles that make up the whole of the jazz dance experience. They also are growing up without exposure to real jazz music - music that swings. (Most of the Congress classes were taught to a pounding techno-aerobic beat). Our dancers are performing a hybrid theatrical movement to pop music, but probably wouldn't know a lindy from a shorty george. Finally, they are being given the impression that jazz dance is only commercial - to entertain or impress. And they are shortchanged in not having exposure to the self discovery and expression that comes from creating in jazz dance.

As I stated earlier, jazz can reveal the spectrum of emotions. But when presented commercially, jazz dance tends to show only a few colors of the rainbow. There is the look at the impressive technical feats dance. There is the get down, get funky dance. There is the wow, it feels great to be a jazz dancer dance. There is the obviously overdone sorrow dance. And there is the let's be a little goofy and comical dance. These approaches are fine for commercial dances of short duration, and for a friendly and forgiving audience, but they will not advance jazz dance as an expressive art form. Here we are at Kennedy Center - why not take advantage of this unique situation and show that jazz dance companies can be on par with modern and ballet companies. To do this our dances need concepts that reach beyond the standard jazz dance deck of choices. Choreographers must think past a five or seven minute time span. And the emotional shadings that jazz musicians have been improvising for decades must be explored as sources for great jazz dances.

We need artists in jazz dance. We need more choreographers like Billy Siegenfeld, a professor from Northwestern University who has developed a unique style he calls classic jazz. Within his brand of movement are the vestiges of Fred Astaire, early Bob Fosse, and the Nicholas Brothers. There are the surprising syncopations of Monk and Bird, and the propulsive rebound from the great swing bands. Siegenfeld's movement recalls the best qualities of jazz music and dance, but is absorbed, digested, and re-invented in a look that is instantly recognizable as his. And importantly, there appears to be a particular motivation for each movement. The choice of movement springs from the thought of what exactly needs to be said at that point in time. No gymnastic - like passes culminating in a switch split here. No maudlin displays of syrupy sentimentality. And he makes dances where women are noteworthy for their style and expressive ability, not their revealing costumes. But that's another subject.

I'm not advocating the complete abandonment of the commercial applications of jazz dance. It's what drives the industry and the reason for much of its existence. But let's not forget that jazz dance came not from television and videos, but from the people responding to music from the soul in a natural way. Jazz dance blossomed in small social gatherings, where dancing from a unique perspective was encouraged. It is our responsibility to set aside some portion of our dancer's training and performing experience to relive that experience and keep it as part of our jazz dance persona. Educators need to schedule workshops in vernacular dance, the lindy, classic Broadway styles like Fosse, Cole, and Robbins, and in feeling and understanding jazz music. Our jazz choreographers need more knowledge in methods of artistic expression, and should be challenged to look beyond the surface of typical jazz concepts. Just as importantly, they need a place to present this type of work, free from the confining financial pressures of commercialism. But then, any dance company, modern or ballet, could benefit from some of these ideas.

I wish I could have been available to see the remaining three nights of concerts, as I missed two pieces by Gus Giordano Jazz Dance Chicago and a Spectrum Dance Theater piece choreographed by Ann Reinking that promised to be more artistic in approach. Perhaps I would have felt differently about some of the Congress, but I think that I still would have liked to see more of our best examples of jazz dance up there with the present examples. How about the Ballet Jazz de Montreal, for whom Buzz Miller choreographed a tribute to Jack Cole, or a jazz dance by the Alvin Ailey Repertory Ensemble? Talley Beatty has jazz pieces performed by Ballet Hispanico, or get a touring show of Jerome Robbins's *West Side Story* to send *Cool*. Frankie Manning could teach a lindy, and since Ann Reinking was a Jazz Dance Congress Award recipient, why not a class in Fosse style? A few of these entrees would have gone a long way toward filling out a sizzling but overly short Jazz Dance World Congress menu.

14

4
BENNY BELL
DANCING WITH CONVICTION AND FREEDOM

Reprinted from *Dancer* with permission, Copyright October 1996

Jazz dance, more than other forms of artistic dance, responds to contemporary culture and music influences by absorbing new trends and ideas. This assimilation of what's hot causes today's jazz dance to be markedly different from that of two decades ago and two centuries ago. As the form reinvents itself, the latest version will eventually seem barely related to the original. So much so that the current model loses the excitement and energy that the original possessed and deteriorates into a bland, distant cousin. This is the feeling of Afro-American jazz dance teacher/ choreographer/ performer Benny Bell, a jazz master who recently taught classes at the 1996 Jazz Dance Congress in Washington, D.C.

Bell gave a historical example of how jazz dance changes to back up his contentions that it has lost its sincerity. In the 1800s, when white Americans saw African slaves dancing a movement that imitated say, chopping wood, the whites only copied the movement but not the motivation behind it. It became just a step ball change, with a comic caricature added onto it. As it was performed in minstrel shows, the presentation was for the enjoyment of the audience. In its original form, the intention was to tell a story of the day's activities and provide a communal experience for the dancers. So the meaning was lost, and the misrepresentation of the movement survived. As this has happened repeatedly over the years, Bell feels that jazz dance has lost its connection to its source and ultimately dropped in quality and sincerity.

Bell's form of jazz dance is about the power and spectacle of African movement. He defines his style as Afro-American, as it is drawn from the African tradition but presented in an American context. He says that in traditional African dance, a tribe might dance for three hours in order to reach a level of emotion where the dancer would attain the end result of transformation of self, the time of projection of peak levels of energy and power. Bell has developed a style that reaches for that peak level without the traditional African process. What most European and Americans want is that power that comes from the result. "What I am busy with is how to add that magic into the technical dance that is already in Europe and America."

Although he has extensively studied Katherine Dunham's technique, Bell's classes reflect his own ideas on dance. They draw from the Dunham idiom, but they can change in relation to the technical levels of his students. At the Jazz Dance Congress, he chose a call and response formula, where he simply demonstrated movement phrases and let the students rely on their own skills in order to emulate him.

From the start, it was obvious that his movement involved skills that American students do not practice in their jazz classes. Bell's torso undulated in a body ripple that began in the mid chest and flowed in waves through the upper spine, into the arms and out the fingers, giving the impression of a bird in flight. In fact, much of his movement had animal traits, whether like a bird or a cat. The students seemed ingrained in the balletic idea of a strong uplifted spine, so the relaxation and trust necessary to allow for the ripple was missing. Another quality that was foreign to the students was the enormous strength and power that came from his dancing in a deep *plie*, and his aggressive attack. Again, students comfortable with straight legs and turns in *releve* quickly tired from dancing in a grounded level.

The physical weakness of many students, and their lack of stamina was a sticking point in Bell's critique of today's jazz dance training. In Europe, Bell contends that he can teach only one hour classes, and that American dancers are slightly better. He recalled two hour classes in the Dunham technique, where the fifteen minute floor section was about strength building exercises. There was no four sets of 8 stretching, and then time for a break and a drink. It was highly physical work, and it created warrior-like dancers who could repeatedly execute the demands of African movement.

Perhaps the deepest chasm between Bell and his students was philosophical. When he danced, it appeared that he was absorbed in his own movements, and that his dance experience was inward and self contained. This contrasted with other classes at the Congress, where class combinations were designed with a watchful audience in mind. He cautioned the students to not worry about how they looked, or to be concerned with the exact placement of an arm or leg. It was more important to arouse a feeling within the body, and then consciously explore, expand, and enjoy that feeling. The reason for movement was self enjoyment and expression, as if no one was watching. This contrasts markedly with most popular jazz dance presentations, where the reason for the movement is to please the audience, or in dance competitions, where favorable response from judges governs the dancer's actions.

Another philosophical idea that Bell pointed out is that all African movement has a specific motivation, while much of what is called jazz dance today is what he calls "preparation for movement." African movement gains impact and truthfulness because it is an imitation of everyday life, like chopping wood or searching for food, or a plea to the gods for a desired outcome - "We are doing this because tomorrow we want sun."

Bell said that he noticed that much of the choreography presented at the Congress was movement without purpose.

"What I hate is that there are so many rules about who can do so many turns, how high is the leg, how high is that jump. That shouldn't matter. Ballet and jazz are storytelling devices. They should be evoking some emotional thing. So if within that emotional thing you ask for three pirouettes - that shouldn't happen. I shouldn't see 'OK, the preparation, and three turns.' It's all a preparation for, but it's not about."

Bell elaborated when he said that motivation:

."...is the difference and the element that has been stripped away and is missing from jazz dance - where is the soul, and why are you doing it."

17

He continued with:

"All the movement is natural, and it comes from a point. Your job is to find that point - it's a point of conviction and freedom at the same time."

The freedom comes from the fire and energy that is liberated from the soul, which radiates in waves from the mid torso through the body and arms. The conviction is the respect for and belief in this dance expression. For him it is so deep that he refuses to compromise in the face of today's commercial pressures.

"In our profession we are like slaves - 'oh my god, we've got to keep the numbers up, or they're going to go to aerobics!' They have made us virtually doormats. And I say if I have to be a doormat, I will be nothing at all. And I say 'Here's your money - get out! Because this is what I do."

Bell hinted at the difference in respect for the art form between ballet and jazz dancers when he said:

"If somebody is going to do Giselle, you do it properly or you don't do it at all. We also have to say 'This is what jazz dance is, these are the elements of jazz dance. Either you do this, or you don't do jazz dance.' As jazz teachers, we've got to get back there."

Obviously the public recognizes something special and moving in his movement, as his teaching at the Congress widened the experience of all who took his class. In Europe, his classes are filled, his company *African Moves* is well received, and he enjoys a busy schedule teaching in dance and academic schools. His plan for the future is to open his own school in Holland, where he will train others to be teachers in his Afro-American style. He hopes that all jazz dancers, whether concert, street, or show dancers, will adopt his philosophy of dancing with conviction and freedom. Only then will jazz dance flourish and reach higher levels of expression and acceptance.

5
PAUL DRAPER – AN ARTIST AND A GENIUS

Reprinted from *Dancer* with permission, Copyright December 1996

On Friday, September 20, 1996, not only the dance community but the entire world of artistic expression lost a unique individual - one who insisted on finding his own means of expression and forged a career that still bears its imprint on styles of tap dance today. At the age of eight-six, the tap dancer Paul Draper succumbed to emphysema in Woodstock, NY.

Many young tap and jazz dancers are not well versed on the subject of tap dance history, and may not know of any famous tappers beyond Savion Glover and Gregory Hines. But in his heyday in the 1940s, Paul Draper's notoriety equaled that of today's exponents, while his artistry still remains unexcelled. Draper's success in combining the disciplines of tap dance and ballet, crafted with his highly developed aesthetic taste, propelled him to the forefront of vaudeville, concert, and film performances.

Draper was raised in an atmosphere of European culture. Born in Italy of American parents in 1909, his father was a professional singer and his mother a patron of the arts. His aunt, Muriel Draper, was a world renowned monologist. In a documentary on Paul Draper produced by the American Dance Machine, Draper recounts being awakened at three in the morning as his parents entertained musical greats like Arthur Rubenstein and other renowned contemporaries. From this classical beginnings, Draper moved on to the music and dance of the day - jazz and tap dance.

After working as a ballroom dance instructor at an early age, Draper picked up a few tap steps from a friend and brashly invented his own routines with the goal of becoming a professional tap dancer. He spent some time touring in Europe, dancing to jazz music, before he returned to NY with the idea of somehow tapping to classical music. With the aid of his mother, who knew George Balanchine personally, Draper enrolled at the new School of American Ballet in 1933 and found himself, at the age of 23, in classes with nine and ten year olds. The ballet sensibility he acquired was sufficient to allow him to literally invent a new branch of tap dancing - tapping to classical music. The use of the upper body and arms in balletic port de bras accompanied a lighter approach to footwork. Tap dancers of the day strove to "lay down iron," or to make heavy sounds. Draper's use of classical music forced him to soften his sounds. He had to rethink the traditional tap shoe - and he used a very thin, small tap on the toe and a half moon tap on the heels. On the toe, he would file the tap down to be paper thin, and compare the sounds of the two toe taps so that they would sound exactly alike.

After gaining recognition in elegant niteclubs across the nation, Draper found himself in a few movies but really found his niche on the concert stage. (On an A & E presentation of the movie *Blue Skies* with Fred Astaire and Bing Crosby, the host Nick Clooney mentioned that Paul Draper was originally cast in the Astaire role, but was fired due to complications - most likely Draper was being too artistic for Hollywood tastes). In places like NY's Carnegie Hall, Draper gave solo concerts in tap dance or teamed up with partner Larry Adler, who played classical music on the harmonica. Their act was tremendously successful, and for nearly a decade they grossed over $100,000 per year, an unheard of sum for nearly any show biz act, much less a concert act. Their careers came to a grinding halt in the 1950s, however, as the pair were accused of being communist sympathizers in the McCarthy era. The act split up, and Draper, at the height of his ability, moved to Switzerland.

Eventually, with a freer political climate, Draper returned to America and became a professor at Carnegie-Mellon in Pittsburgh. His approach to tap was revered but not really practiced by those who led the resurgence of tap dancing in the 1970s. Thanks to the foresight of Lee Theodore, director of the American Dance Machine, Draper was commissioned by the company to teach two months of classes and choreograph a tap piece in November and December of 1979. During this workshop, company members preserved the Draper style in a Tap Concerto in three movements, and many dancers experienced and absorbed not only the technique but the artistry of Paul Draper. I know, because I was one of the lucky few.

At that time I was a beginning tap student, armed with an arsenal of not much more than a time step and a flap ball change. I was keen with anticipation of classes with a legend of tap dance, but really ignorant of Draper's approach and format. Coming from a class here and there of six time steps and a break, Draper's technique and class was like a 180 degree turn. After a general body warmup, I found myself at the *barre* performing plies in tap shoes, flap *tendus* from fifth position in tap shoes, *frappes en croix* in tap shoes, *ronde jambe enlair* with heel drops in tap shoes - you name it, Draper had the ballet *barre* adapted to accommodate the footwork and rhythmic application of tap. It was a full body approach, with arms and *epaulement*. Then, there were the double pullbacks at the *barre*. Not moving backwards on the pullback, but with the goal of more or less tapping the feet in one spot so that the pullback could be performed without movement, or moving back or sides or crossing the feet, and even forward. Wings were pursued in inventive patterns, a favorite of his being a flap heel on the right, a brush diagonal on the left, a wing and heel on the right, a step heel on the left, and a toe of the right foot hitting the floor behind the left heel. This was performed in a constant stream of sound that never failed to make tap dancers as well as non-tap dancers sit forward to see where all of those sounds came from.

The center floor work was just as precise, with attention given to dynamic shading of sounds as well as the appearance of the full body. As Draper explained in the ADM documentary, he wanted his feet to be light and part of the overall presentation of the body. He avoided making the feet predominate, as in traditional forms of tap. And I never imagined that there could be so many ways of executing a waltz clog, but Paul had variation after variation.

Although the two month workshop vastly improved my tap technique, I think that the most notable aspect of the Draper experience was just being in the presence of Draper as an artist. Listening to him expound on what makes tap dancing an art as opposed to mechanics challenged all of us to look beyond technique and find the reason to dance. In the documentary, Draper clearly states that tap dancing is relatively simple to master - there is a toe, a heel, a brush, a scrape out and flap in, and a toe heel. That can all be mastered in about six months of arduous application. But after that, a person would still not know how to *dance*. For Draper, "to dance is to move in such fashion that another human being will understand something about his or her relationship to the rest of the world that they previously had not understood." His movements had a clear motivation, to communicate to an audience as well as entertain, and that leads to why ultimately Draper is unique, a genius. In order to facilitate his desire to communicate his personal vision, he looked around him and used what was in front of him - tap and ballet- to invent a new medium of expression. As Bob Fosse states in the ADM documentary "Paul Draper was the first and in subsequent years, had many imitators - but none who could equal his artistry ...There is no doubt about it, Paul Draper affected everyone's style."

I had two months of classes with Paul Draper, more than seventeen years ago, but the influence of Draper is still with me today. I do not teach his *barre*, but I am imbued with his dynamic and aural approach to tap dancing. I still teach many of his center floor combinations, which are so pure and beneficial to students that they will be relevant to students of tap dancing a hundred years from now. I strive for the clarity and musicality that he seemed to achieve so effortlessly. And, yes, I give my own many versions of the waltz clog. I look to him as a role model, remembering him at age 71, out-dancing students fifty years younger than him. (Although he would discount this statement - Draper felt that you do not do something in spite of your age - "either you do the thing or you don't do the thing.")

I feel sorry for tap dancers who have now will never grow from exposure to the Draper style and artistry. Paul Draper was an artistic genius, and I, for one, am glad that he chose tap dancing as the means for expressing his unique vision. One of the dancers in the documentary states that Paul Draper "made tap dancing some alive for me." Paul Draper made tap dancing come alive for me also. I would encourage all students of tap to seek out information on Draper and learn from his example.

**The American Dance Machine Documentary on Paul Draper was first aired on PBS in 1980. It is available at the Dance Collection at the Library at Lincoln Center in New York, but I believe that is now available commercially. For more information on Paul Draper, you may be able to find his book, *On Tap*, or you may search issues of *Dance Magazine* from the 1950s and 1960s when he wrote a column on tap dance. There is also a chapter on Paul Draper in Rusty Frank's book *Tap - The Greatest Tap Dance Stars and Their Stories*. Draper appeared in the movies *Colleen* (1936) and *The Time of Your Life* (1948).

6
THE CHOREOGRAPHIC PROCESS
IN MUSICAL THEATRE

Reprinted from *Dancer* with permission, Copyright February 1996

The art of choreography is almost as difficult to define as jazz dance. Many from the world of concert dance, particularly modern, have advanced their theories on dance creation and those who create them (the most notable being Doris Humphrey in *The Art of Making Dances*). The world of musical theatre choreography has been less represented in expositions on the choreographic process. That is why a new book, *Conversations with Choreographers*, is so important. In this informative and intriguing collection of interviews, Svetlana McLee Grody and Dorothy Daniels Lister have assembled the history, secrets, and process of many of the top choreographers and director/choreographers in the business. Any dancer or aspiring choreographer interested in the world of musical theatre would do well to wear out the pages of this book.

My first impression was the sharp distinction between concert and musical theatre choreography. Concert choreographers are responsible for inventing and defining the reason or concept for their piece. Their starting point is a blank stage and their personal vision. For the musical theatre choreographer, work is defined (or limited) by the show's plot, characters, music, time period, sets, and the working habits of the rest of the creative team. The concert choreographer has the primary creative responsibility for the piece, whereas the musical theatre choreographer must learn to be part of a collaborative team and work with more restrictions (Wayne Cilento, for one, abhors a blank stage and pleads "Give me obstacles to overcome!").

Like the Humphrey book does for concert dance, *Conversations with Choreographers*, gives insight into the qualities and methods of successful musical theatre choreographers, and many generalizations can be deduced. First, musical theatre choreographers are successful dancers first, and have not studied choreography in schools or other courses. They tend to have creative natures, dating back to when they were first dancing. Tommy Tune would spend his summer vacations staging shows in his backyard with kids from the neighborhood. Michael Bennett cajoled his high school into allowing him to choreograph dances during class time rather than attend academic classes.

Most of the choreographers credited a varied dance background, with an emphasis on ballet, as being vital. They have a knowledge of ballet, jazz, tap, and ballroom, and are willing to learn ethnic styles or bring in experts for particular shows. (This should be a wake up call for dancers today who only study contemporary styles of dance). And all of the choreographers began as dancers first. Most of them were working in the professional world before they were twenty years old. And, importantly, all received their first choreographic assignments after being hired as dancers. Producers and directors tend to know little of dance, and historically have less regard for dance than plot or music in their productions. Respect for the dancer's ability and congeniality are more highly regarded than his or her previous experience. The choreographers all state that they were offered their first jobs by producers they were working for, by recommendations from past dance employment, and in many cases, by accident. To all aspiring choreographers, it is quite clear that entry into the field comes from who you know, not what you know. Initially, your dance ability and networking skills will get you a choreographer's job before your demo tape will.

The final quality of a successful choreographer is an instinctive sense of taste in movement, music, and the musical theatre genre. These choreographers grew up in the field, learning by practical experience and personal observation of the greats. Chris Chadman, Graciela Daniele, and Wayne Cilento credit Fosse. Many were influenced by Michael

Bennett, while almost all cite Jerome Robbins as the epitome of a musical theatre choreographic artist. In terms of music, most did not know how to read or play music, and only a few knew enough to interpret a score. What they do have is an acute musical sensitivity. They know what feelings are projected by different sounds and textures of music, and they could feel when to slip from one time signature to another, one key to another, and how to build a number to a climax. Most worked with dance arrangers to create their own dance music, yet they didn't know how to read music themselves. Their work springs from years of hands on experience in one show a week summer stock assignments and their desire to be knowledgeable in all musical styles (another lesson for aspiring choreographers).

Structured improvisation was cited as the most frequent method for creation of musical theatre dances. Although there is a faction that prefers to work out all choreography in pre-production (Bob Fosse and his protege Chris Chadman and many of the television choreographers), the rest recognize musical theatre as a collaborative process involving directors, composers, designers, and even dancers. By structure, it is meant that the choreographer will lay out a set of defining characteristics and then create movement with those ideas as parameters. The most important are the plot, characters, music, and time period and physical location. After consultation with the rest of the creative team, the choreographer greatly narrows the choice of movement by the limitations imposed. Like a miner searching for gold with a series of finer sieves, the limitations allow the choreographer to choose movement that best fits the overall concept of the musical. Quite often, the remark was made that once the concept was finely tuned, the choice of movement was simple.

Another sense of structure is seen when the choreographer does research into time periods by watching old movies and reviewing old books, postcards, and artwork of earlier decades. The choreographer then maps out a basic plan of attack and choice of movements, but the finished dance is not set. The final limiting factor curiously welcomed by choreographers was a limited amount of rehearsal time. They feel that having a deadline forces them to come to quick decisions, and therefore rely on instinct. Many said that the first version of their dances was usually the best, and that excessive tinkering leads to a dilution of the initial impact. Cleaning and refining of a dance is always desired, but too much time leads to procrastination or variance from the original spark of creativity.

The place where the dance comes together is in rehearsal. These choreographers are nearly unanimous in mentioning the value of working with dancers who have unique personalities and acting abilities. They do not wish to work with dancers who are technically advanced, but who are expressionless. And here is where the improvisation lies. The dances are created with input from the dancers as well as they creative staff. The choreographer operates as an editor as well as a creator of movement. By taking suggestions from dancers, they feel that the dances are enhanced, and a greater texture of performance is evoked. They feel that individual characters can be created in this fashion, leading to a more interesting performance. The dancers look more like themselves, as opposed to the Fosse pre-choreographed method, where dancers all tend to look like various incarnations of Fosse himself.

This aspect of creation was the most enlightening for me. Most dancers, in their formative years, come from dance backgrounds where they are told every step, movement, and position by their teacher or choreographer. This leads to dancers who respond to direction, but who cannot contribute anything of their own. In the service of creating better musical theatre dancers, perhaps we as teachers should devote portions of our rehearsal time to challenging our dancers to assist in creating some dances. It would appear that a dancer/actor will get the musical theatre job before the person who is solely a technical dancer.

So for the aspiring musical theatre dancer or choreographer, the key to success is a knowledge of many dance styles as well as talent as an actor. The ability and desire to participate in improvisation, abhorred by many dancers, is necessary. And years of practical experience culminating in an acquired taste and knowledge of music and the persona of the musical theatre will add to your success and employability. A fine singing voice should go without mention. Dance, acting, voice - a very tall order, indeed. Now, where can our future choreographers and dancers go to develop these skills? It isn't found easily, and is getting harder all the time. Many of the mentioned choreographers learned their craft in those summer theatre sweatshops, where they were challenged to choreograph a full show, in various styles, every week. Daunting work, but the best experience. With the decline in summer theatres, today's dancers are missing out on this vital proving ground. That's why *Conversations with Choreographers* is such a valuable tool. Lifetimes of musical theatre wisdom are compressed into one easy reading volume. This book and its lessons are a must for anyone desiring a career in the American musical theatre.

7
JAZZ DANCE AMERICA
THE SPECTRUM OF JAZZ DANCE

Reprinted from *Dancer* with permission, Copyright March 1997

Jazz dance is a multi-faceted thing - absorbing and incorporating influences from all aspects of dance. That is why a concert jazz dance company is the perfect place for Maurice Brandon Curry, an innovative choreographer-teacher-producer. After having directed and choreographed such diverse projects as the Tour de France, Italian television shows, off-Broadway shows, and videos for the artist formerly known as Prince; staged shows for Barbra Streisand and Diana Ross; and directed ballet companies and taught throughout the country, Curry decided that he needed "his own sandbox' to play in - and Jazz Dance America was born.

That was five years ago, and in that time Curry's Jazz Dance America has accomplished a seemingly impossible task - becoming firmly established as a New York based concert jazz dance company. You would think that in New York City, the home of the Broadway jazz of Cole and Kidd and jazz music meccas like the Savoy Ballroom and Birdland, would enjoy a rich landscape of jazz dancing. But Cole and Kidd are gone, and so are the clubs where jazz music was born and developed. Maurice Brandon Curry saw a need for entertaining jazz dance in the jazz music capital, and his enthusiasm and passion have given an alternative to the angst and victim art of the city's culturally elite.

31

For Curry, jazz dance is uplifting and without bounds. The company's stated goal is to present jazz dance in all shades, styles, and colors - with an emphasis on American choreographers and composers. He has also taken a belief from Jack Cole, the true father of theatrical jazz dance, who said that, above all, jazz dance must be entertaining. Curry has said "One thing I despise is dancers that have incredible facility and incredible training but you feel nothing when you see them dance. They are dancing for themselves, not for the audience, and that's not what my work is about. My work is about entertaining."

Jazz Dance America took shape the way many companies first do - Curry gathered together friends and, with blind faith, financed and staged a concert. But Curry travels in high places, so his friends include dancers from the Alvin Ailey American Dance Theatre, American Ballet Theatre, the White Oak Project, and Broadway shows. Those associated with performances in the past have included Mercedes Ellington, Tony winner Thommie Walsh, ABT members Ashley Tuttle and Charles Askegard, and Broadway's Kevin Ramsey, and JDA's associate director Ruthlyn Salomons. As for choreographers, he has enlisted many of the top names in New York - Fred Mann, Jeffrey Ferguson, Raymond Harris, Jonathan Riesling, Anita Ashley, Curry himself, and, oh yeah, some guy named Gene Kelly.

The quality of Curry's roster commanded immediate attention, and the company's biggest break came in the form of an offer from the Pace Downtown Theater to be its home theater. Jill Panfel, director of the theatre which is part of the Schimmel Center for the Arts, was searching for a resident jazz dance company. Although they do not produce JDA's concerts, Panfel is able to provide valuable performance space at attractive rental prices. With the promise of a stable home base, Curry has been able to build the future of the company.

As Jazz Dance America is a repertory company, and jazz dance itself is populated by so many styles, Curry does not hold to any individual jazz dance technique for the company. He prefers to use dancers who have solid backgrounds in ballet and modern technique. Rehearsal time is at a minimum - dancers must be able to grasp a variety of styles in a short time, so Curry feels that classical technique is the best common denominator.

Another reason for using dancers from the classical world, Curry feels, is that audiences today, whether attending a ballet or a jazz performance, expect a certain level of technical ability. "The audience expects the Olympics," he states flatly, and he feels that a dancer trained purely in hip hop or commercial jazz dance styles will not be able to satisfy the demands of the choreography or the expectations of the audience. But then, there's that factor of being able to make the technique come alive with performance ability - and Curry counts that as highly as the dancer's technique.

The New York seasons have been extravaganzas, with high profile supporters and choreographers. This past November, the company presented "One Night Only," which was co-sponsored by Tommy Hilfinger, China Grill, Planet Hollywood, and others. Curry has actively courted corporate sponsorship, as the response from state and government funding agencies for a jazz dance company has been dismal. "They either think jazz music, hip hop, MTV, or they think you're Broadway" and therefore not needing public support. But for now, ticket sales and an active corporate sponsorship program have managed to just pay the bills.

The biggest splash of the November concert was the stage debut of Gene Kelly's "Slaughter on Tenth Avenue." Although this piece was originally choreographed by George Balanchine for the 1936 Broadway production of *On Your Toes*, Kelly provided his own choreography for his version in the 1948 film *Words and Music*. It was a tour de force for Kelly and his vivacious partner, Vera Ellen, and Curry felt it odd that the piece was never adapted for the concert stage. He sought out and received permission from Kelly, the dancin' man himself, and Jazz Dance America presented the world stage premiere of Kelly's "Slaughter." It also put JDA in with fine company, as the only other two dance companies in the world having choreography by Gene Kelly are the San Francisco Ballet and the Paris Opera Ballet. The piece, danced by Ruthlyn Salomons and Keith Ramsey, was a smash success.

So how can the company top this? For the March 1997 season, Curry has first of all enlisted Paula Abdul as honorary Chairperson of the event. She signed on after hearing about Kelly's interest in the company. Curry has also commissioned Ray Leeper, winner of the 1996 Jazz Dance World Congress choreography award, to set a piece, as well as Jeffrey Ferguson. Curry himself will choreograph a piece to music by Ella Fitzgerald. The performance is entitled "This Is Jazz," and will be presented from March 20-23 at the Pace Downtown Theatre, Spruce St. between Park Row and Gold St., in New York City. Reservations for "This Is Jazz" can be made by calling 212-346-1715.

As if he doesn't have enough to occupy his time, Curry also teaches for Dance World Academy in New Jersey, where he has started an apprentice company for Jazz Dance America. This group of teenage dancers, will perform two pieces, choreographed by Dance World Academy directors Donna Farinella and Debbie Wolter.

As for the future growth of Jazz Dance America, Curry is working on a new five year plan. Some new projects include commissioned scores from some high profile jazz artists, and even an original musical theatre production. He also is working in association with two other jazz dance companies to share choreography and lower costs. Above all, he is dedicated to an increased presence as a jazz dance company in New York City. Maurice Brandon Curry has made New York City his "sandbox," and, if he has his way, New Yorkers will be admiring his sand castles for a long time to come.

8
BOB FOSSE – *A DANCIN' MAN*

Reprinted from *Dancer* with permission, Copyright April 1997

Bob Fosse is a Broadway dance legend, his work dominating the look of dance musicals from the 1950s thru the 1980s. And now, nearly eleven years after his death, he still continues to rule the Great White Way with the current adaptation of *Chicago*, his 1975 musical that starred Gwen Verdon and Chita Rivera. Although choreographed by his muse Ann Reinking, *Chicago* is staged in the Fosse style of slick, fluid movements, sharp isolations, an aggressive attitude, and above all - rhythm.

But *Chicago*, more acclaimed now than in 1975 and certifiably a phenomenon, may have to move over and make room for another Fosse production. Chet Walker, a musical theatre teacher at NY's Broadway Dance Center and veteran of many Fosse shows, has collaborated with Gwen Verdon on a new project that will tell the full story of Bob Fosse, with Fosse's original choreography.

The working title is *Bob Fosse - A Dancin' Man*. What began not as a tribute but a celebration of the work of Fosse, in the form of a television special, has now become a stage presentation. Walker recently took time off from his schedule of daily classes at Broadway Dance Center to discuss designing a show about the man who shaped the careers of so many, and his conception of the work.

Chet Walker

Walker debuted on Broadway in *Pippin* at the age of 16. He was a ballet dancer, with no idea of jazz style or isolation, and although he felt totally inadequate, Fosse would not give up on him. Under Fosse's direction, Walker became a repository of the Fosse style, and was a primary performer in Fosse's 1978 production of *Dancin'*. As a way to say thank you from the multitude of dancers Fosse created as well as himself, Walker decided to assemble the best of Fosse's work in various media - film, television, and stage. "I brought him the idea of creating a company that he didn't have to be involved in, unless he wanted to. I wanted to recreate all of his work. I wanted to have a catalog. I created two books and presented it to him. He laughed and looked through all of it, and said 'Do you think that anyone is really interested in this?'"

Obviously, people are interested in Bob Fosse. To the point that his associates continue to work in his style with great success. Walker's dilemma was in choosing which form the project should take. After Fosse died in 1987, he dropped the idea and let it rest. But after a few years, he revived it in the form of a stage presentation. With a cast of 26 dancers, it would show the evolution of Bob Fosse from his beginnings as a young film star in the image of Fred Astaire, through his classic and comic period of the 1960s, to the high powered dance extravaganzas of the 1970s, and up to the final version of the Fosse style that Walker calls "the dark period."

On the subject of the scope of Fosse's work, Walker says "there are so many years that people don't know about. Most will look at what I call the dark period. It's sensual, the style moved to a very oily, slithery, percussive one - a lot of dark costumes - and the subject matter of some of those musicals were darker than *The Pajama Game*. What people don't know about are the television stuff, the movies, *The Adventures of Dobie*

Gillis, My Sister Eileen, these kind of shows that are so white and so pastel and so charming, and he is adorable as an actor." Walker singled out dances like "Herby Fitch's Twitch," "Real Live Girl," "I've Got Your Number," and "Mu Cha Cha" as examples of Fosse's early playful innocence and strong sense of comedy. These are the dances that people do not think of when the name Fosse is mentioned, but must be examined in order to know all aspects of his style.

He explained that the style is so complex that a dancer cannot learn the mechanics of the style as well as the enormous amount of choreography in a short rehearsal period. To get the project going and develop dancers, he first gave free classes in Fosse's style. Once into rehearsal, he touched on 34 Fosse dances in just 21 days.

Walker's celebration of the choreography of Bob Fosse has been presented in Toronto, where he was able to find crucial financial backing and producers. The structure of the performance itself is still being shaped, and Walker could not put it into a standard category. "We created this 'thing.' It's not a musical, it's not a dance musical. It's like *Dancin'* in that it's a musical entertainment. It's to show his choreography. But it is not a retrospective of shows that he did."

When pressed for an explanation of why another Fosse show, Walker had three reasons. First, to thank Fosse for blessing the theatre, audiences, and so many dancers with his genius. Fosse's work touched millions, and he deserves the attention normally given to other serious dance artists. Second, a need for an accurate telling of the Fosse story - all aspects of his choreography and the evolution of his style.

Third, Walker feels that a Fosse show would be an excellent tool to spark a rebirth in the traditional musical theatre dancer. He feels that attitudes and methods of training have changed in the last two decades to the point that the true musical theatre dancer is nearly extinct. One shortcoming he feels strongly about is philosophical. "In the present generation, you want to get it - get it and move on. I come from a generation where that's not true. You were constantly striving to get it. You held the idea that the dancer could always do better and worked constantly to improve. Mr. Fosse would say in *Dancin'*, for example, if you ever thought you did a perfect show, you should really hand in your notice. It's impossible {to do a perfect show}, and that's kind of cool, to keep working to perfection."

To be a successful Fosse dancer, Walker feels that you must be trained in many areas, not just dance. First, a strong ballet technique. Acrobatic ability is important, as well as knowledge of many styles of jazz dance and dance periods. Some tap is helpful, especially rhythm tap as opposed to show tap. You have to sing, and you have to be able to express yourself and work from an actor's point of view. "Mr. Fosse didn't do steps for steps sake. There was a purpose. Each step had a reason behind it, that had to be brought out...when you go to acting class, learn to apply it to your dancing - don't leave it in acting."

As for the future, Walker's celebration of Bob Fosse is in pre-production for a fall 1997 opening. It may not be in NY, but the backing is in place, so it should be on the boards somewhere this fall. Chet Walker's project is a much needed lesson about Bob Fosse, the creator of the most recognizable and visible Broadway jazz dance style. Younger dancers need to see this show to learn where musical theatre dance came from, and what it should be. And all dancers, performers, and audience members need to see this show just to pay their respects and say thank you to Bob Fosse - the quintessential Broadway *Dancin' Man*.

9
JAZZ DANCE MAVERICK
DANNY BURACZESKI

Reprinted from *Dancer* with permission, Copyright May 1997

Like the comedian Rodney Dangerfield, jazz dance companies and choreographers often complain that, from the artistic dance establishment, they don't get any respect. Funding agencies and concert dancers dismiss the "hard sell" approach of many jazz dance performances, leaving the pot of grant money to be handed over to ballet and modern companies. Some jazz dance companies look to corporate sponsorship or even bypass the standard non-profit status and run their companies as for-profit corporations, forgoing any opportunity to seek funding. However, one unique jazz dance choreographer has combined the choreographic approach of modern dance with the rhythms and feel of jazz music, and in the process has gained a nod of approval from foundations, arts organizations, and dance critics across the nation. JAZZDANCE by Danny Buraczeski (pronounced bu-ra-CHESS-kee) has received favorable reviews from the NY Times and other papers across the country. After a highly successful stay at NY's prestigious Joyce Theatre in 1995, the company will return this year from May 13-18 for a second week long engagement.

Buraczeski began to dance at Bucknell University in Pennsylvania, and soon found himself on Broadway in *Mame* and *The Act* with Liza Minelli. His first effort as a choreographer came in two self produced concerts in New York City in 1979. In 1989 he left for Minneapolis and a co-directorship of the Zenon Dance Company. In 1992 he split from Zenon, forming JAZZDANCE as a solitary outlet for his jazz dance choreography, and since then has built the company

into an international touring group, now consisting of nine dancers. He receives funding from four foundations, and from city and state arts organizations, and he feels that the label of "jazz dance company" is a not a liability.

After a performance at Penn State University in March, 1997, Buraczeski elaborated on the quick success of his jazz dance company, and its acceptance by the dance establishment. The key, he feels, is in his artistic approach and his abstention from the hard sell, or entertainment value of typical jazz dance performances. Buraczeski says that his dances are "intelligent, self-contained, and fully realized - they are complete in themselves." Jazz music is his inspiration and starting point, and each different piece of music will inspire a new movement vocabulary. He is not content to rely on standard jazz movements, but would rather take ideas suggested by the music and shape them into movements that are tailored to the need of the individual dance.

Buraczeski is quick to point out that he likes all forms of dance, and has studied ballet, modern, and tap. He credits Betsy Haug, who was influenced by Henry LeTang, as developing his appreciation and knowledge of the traditional jazz dance idiom. "At that time, in the 1970s, she was the only one using real jazz music." But his approach to the structure of a dance is more from the modern dance heritage than the "knock 'em dead" notion of commercial jazz dance. Buraczeski loves "design - the architecture, and making up a new vocabulary for each suite of music. I will agonize over making the design element just right." The choreographer is unusual in having the facilities and time to agonize. While most artists face rehearsal and space constraints, Buraczeski has negotiated an arrangement with a ballet school in Minneapolis where he receives virtual free reign during day time hours in return for making some dances for the school's professional program. With an abundance of time, he can then work slowly and carefully, trying movement ideas on his dancers without a constant eye on the clock. This rare abundance of choreographic resources has given him the opportunity to formulate his jazz dance aesthetic.

As for dancers, Buraczeski does not look for a specific technique or dance background. Instead he looks for dancers who have "musicality, rhythmic clarity, versatility, as eclectic a background as possible, and a  strong set of lungs - as my work is very aerobic! I like dancers who are grounded, who don't mind spending two hours in *plié*, and all of my dancers look different - I don't want carbon copies of each other." Buraczeski describes himself as a "stylist" rather than a technician, and he demands dancers who have, above all, a well developed musicality and rhythmic awareness.

"Swing Concerto" is rapidly becoming his signature dance piece, and will be performed at the upcoming Joyce engagement. This piece, as well as his other work, has been described as "downright terrific...extraordinary and energetic" by Anna Kisselgoff of the *New York Times*, "...high polish, full of style and energy..." by Clive Barnes of the *New York Post*, and "scintillating..." by Marilyn Tucker of the *San Francisco Chronicle*. Joe Mazo, the late critic for *Dance Magazine* and the

Bergen Record, wrote that "Buraczeski is that rarity, a true jazz choreographer. He takes the rhythms and makes them the basis of his choreography. The movement is full of surprises and inventive structures, but for Buraczeski, steps are only the medium; the music is the message."

Buraczeski will also premiere two new pieces, "Bone Matter" and "Among These Cares." The first is a blues dance, a tribute to the Kansas City Blues. The second involves a rare item in the world of jazz dance - a commissioned jazz score. The Kennedy Center for the Arts asked Burazceski to work with a jazz composer on a new work, and his choice was the pianist Sir Roland Hanna. Buraczeski had always admired Hanna'a combination of jazz classicism, rhythm, and melody, and the two set to work on a new concert jazz dance. Buraczeski mentioned that he wanted to make a dance about family and memories, and the composer responded with a score in the sonata form for violin and piano.

For "Among These Cares," Buraczeski will make use of an elaborate stage design - a set of five Roman shades, each containing seven images, that twist and turn to reveal a variety of settings. Designed by Susan Weil, the shades in places contain silk screened images of the choreographer's mother. The piece also has costumes by Mary Hansmeyer, and will be performed with live accompaniment.

Running any dance company is a tough proposition, and jazz companies are always the last in line for respect and attention, but Buraczeski thrives on the chance to create movement in the jazz dance idiom. He has taken a seeming liability and turned it into his supreme advantage - a uniqueness stemming from his artistic treatment of jazz music and jazz dance. The response to his company is always eye-opening, and he mentioned the remarks of a modern dancer who just experienced his company at Penn State. "She was not looking forward to a 'jazz dance' company, but was thrilled with what she saw and what could be done with jazz." Buraczeski said that "people seem openly glad that I am doing this," and that the "doorway {to success} is the fact that I use jazz music." Although it would seem logical, a jazz dance company performing to jazz music in an artistic fashion is not the standard perception of the dance establishment. But JAZZDANCE by Danny Buraczeski, by looking to the classic forms of jazz music and jazz dance as inspiration, is bucking the trend and changing the way people look and feel about jazz dance. JAZZDANCE by Danny Buraczeski will perform at The Joyce Theatre, 175 Eighth Ave, New York, NY, from May 13 - 18, 1997. For tickets call 212-242-0800.

**Photo credits - Photo #1 – Roy Blakey, Photos #2 & #3 – Alvis Upitis, Photo #4 – Jack Mitchell.

10
JAZZ DANCE AESTHETIC AND PHILOSOPHY

Reprinted from *Dancer* with permission, Copyright June 1997

As dancers, we spend an inordinate number of hours practicing and laboring at our craft. A lifetime of sore muscles and bodies drenched with sweat, all in the pursuit of a career as a dancer, teacher, or choreographer. Dancers pay their dues, putting in hours far beyond what "normal" people devote to their jobs, to the exclusion of many of the simpler joys of life that most people seem to take for granted. We are compulsive - in many cases obsessive - in our desire to attain a position in life where we can "dance." So, if we as dancers are willing to devote ourselves and completely sacrifice aspects of life as we know it, what guarantee is there that we can receive our long awaited rewards?

Well, as far as I know, there isn't any. Like the old saying says, there is a broken heart for every light on Broadway. Its a business where supply far exceeds demand, and hundreds of dancers applying for four slots at a Broadway audition is the norm. Rejection is expected, and depression is commonplace. We begin to think "What is wrong with me? Why can't I dance?"

My thought is not that there is something wrong with us, but that we all too often look for satisfaction in dance in the wrong places. To allow your self-worth as a dancer and a person to be judged by a casting agent or competition judge is wrong. It's a moment in time, a snap decision by someone who has observed you for as little as a few seconds. Their decision not to use or praise you, although often truthfully based on an honest evaluation of ability, can many times be based on a personal preference as to height, hair color, or body shape. Nothing wrong with you at that moment - you just weren't the flavor of the day.

But you are still depressed you were rejected, and mad that you don't have the dance job, what you think is the real "determination" of your worth as a dancer. And as jazz dancers, primarily working in the commercial sphere, we tend to measure ourselves against unattainable standards presented by the media and the cutthroat competition of dance auditions. What I propose is that, instead of defining success as jazz dancers by the audition process, let's value our jazz dance experience by what we say as artists and not by how many accolades are bestowed on us. We must devise a better philosophy as to why a jazz dancer dances.

This means that, instead of thinking of the rewards we get from dance as measured solely in ribbons and trophies or auditions won, think of how we can serve a vision of dance that is greater than ourselves. Think of the personal satisfaction of dance expression, real expression from one person to another that becomes art in the truest sense of the word. Art has the unique dichotomy of simultaneously having no value, and value that is inestimable. The value is in the hearts and minds of those who experience it, and no casting director or judge can take that away from you. To dance in this fashion makes your dance experience real and truthful, springing from the sincerity of your actions.

Some of my thoughts are guided by an event that the renowned critic Deborah Jowitt described in a recent article in *Dance Magazine*. She told of how the noted choreographer Anna Sokolow was setting a piece on a group of college students. They were not rising to her expectations, and in an attempt to enhance their performance, she raised her voice and threw a chair at them as they danced across the floor, exhorting them to a higher level. Many students were shocked and upset by her behavior. Sokolow calmed their fears by saying "It's not that I hate you, but that I love dance more than I love you."

That single sentence contains a lifetime of philosophical advice to all jazz dancers. It tells us that "dance" is something to be respected and placed above our own personal aspirations. It means that when we dance, we should approach it with a reverence and a desire to bring ourselves to a higher standard, and that if we do not push ourselves to reach that standard, we would be better off to abandon our efforts entirely. Dance should be something we love, that we do all the way, all of the time. And when we do, we should get satisfaction from our own personal critique of our efforts and accomplishments, not solely from the cursory opinions of others.

The reason for dancing by many in jazz dance is a sure fire way to experience depression. Our dancing is not connected to the soul, to our intrinsic involvement. The reason we dance needs to be adjusted. Enlightened. We need to adopt a new philosophy in jazz dance. I feel that I have been helped tremendously in my approach to dance in jazz by searching for advice, listening to great artists, and by learning more about the true meaning of jazz dance.

First, there is Paul Draper, who was a tap dancer, knowledgeable in jazz dance, with an artistic temperament. He defined the distinction between "dance steps" and "dancing" when he said that tap had about six basic sounds, and a dancer could learn them in about six months of practice. But then, the dancer still would not know what it means "to dance." Draper said "To dance is to move in such fashion as to make another human being understand something about the relationship of their self to the universe that he previously didn't understand." Draper felt that merely performing steps was not "dancing," and that to connect the movement to an idea or feeling makes the dancer an artist, not just a body moving through space. Connecting our external movements to inner thoughts brings a deeper meaning.

Then there is Erick Hawkins, speaking of the contributions of Martha Graham in *Martha Graham - The Evolution Of Her Dance Theory and Training 1926 - 1991*, compiled by Marian Horosko. Hawkins said that Graham established an aesthetic in modern dance, and goes on to say that for the highest quality dance:

An aesthetic vision has to be present - a desirable goal that is not based upon gaining notoriety, money, or acceptability - but is based upon reaching the aesthetic vision. That doesn't mean starving, but it does mean that a group or a dancer has to have a standard, a level, a goal that is beyond the demands of the general culture.

There is a lot of competition in dance, so many more people in dance than ever before, and not a great deal of good judgment in the people who make dance possible. Razz-ma-tazz has found an audience. People are dancing for the wrong reasons. I think our generation danced because we only had one reason: the desire to dance to an aesthetic goal. That was satisfaction enough. I'm not talking about art for art's sake, but for being honest in the reasons for dancing and for creating dances. For Hawkins and others of his time, achieving the desired level of aesthetic standard provided all of the positive reinforcement they needed.

The jazz critic Roger Pryor Dodge has given me tremendous enlightenment about the evolution of jazz dance and music in the 1920s and 1930s. Writing in *Hot Jazz and Jazz Dance*, Dodge outlines the personalities of various jazz musicians. Musicians who improvise heartfelt solos, blistering or bluesy, and then live for the next moment of impassioned jazz expression. They do not attempt to write it down, analyze it, judge it, or rate it - they just do it and find satisfaction in making it happen. If it feels right, and it flows from the heart, then its good. And that is where they find their primary level of justification in their actions. Of course, the secondary level of making a living at their craft is there, as it is here for dancers today. And that judgment is a real one, as we all have to survive. But these musicians knew that the feeling from the music was the main thing. Just as the feelings evoked through jazz dance must be the main thing.

I think that this is a major challenge to jazz dancers - to find ways to bring more artistic expression to our craft. If a movement doesn't have a motivation, it is merely a shell, a technical calisthenic. As dancers performing that kind of movement, we feel empty too. We look to others to give us value. Whether in concerts or competitions, jazz dancers need to find ways to incorporate motivation for movements into all choreography. And we must approach every performance, every class, and every rehearsal with the respect for the art of dance and the desire to execute and experience it on the highest level. It takes concentration and it takes focus. And it takes having a clear understanding and vision of what art is, and what artistic expression in jazz dance is. It takes having an aesthetic and a philosophy about jazz dance, as Erick Hawkins said, is "beyond the demands of the general culture." When jazz dancers can acquire that, jazz and jazz dancers will be on their way to achieving their potential and finding a lasting satisfaction and worth in jazz dance.

11
SHARING THE PASSION –
JAZZ DANCE L.A. 1997

Reprinted from *Dancer* with permission, Copyright July 1997

Los Angeles - home of Hollywood, television, and the 3 second cutaway - has not been noted for having a deep respect for the expressive arts. Rather, the City of Angels is a place for the trendiest, hottest, and flashiest types of entertainment. But within this land of "the look" lurks a dedicated group of artistic jazz dancers. Due to their efforts, in the form of a non profit organization named *Jazz Dance L.A.*, concert styles of jazz dance are presented in a yearly performance that has drawn not only the best of L.A., but performers of international stature.

Although *Jazz Dance L.A.* launched its first concert in 1994, its history goes back to Tokyo, Japan, and a young dancer named Hama.

 From 1959 - 1964, Hama was a leading dancer in a Japanese variety show. He became interested in American jazz dance and came to New York, studying extensively with Luigi. Soon his assistant, Hama taught at Luigi's Dance Center and performed on Broadway. By the early 70s, though, Hama was back in California, where he taught, choreographed, and performed in television variety shows. During that time Hama was known as a "Luigi" dancer to the dance world, but his methods and style were changing, becoming more of an expression of his own dance experience. "I couldn't shake it off," he says of the reputation, " but I had to get off of his style. I wanted to expand it, and I challenged it. But

his philosophy- to not pound the body - that I have kept." In 1991 Hama's influence on the dance scene of Los Angeles culminated in the opening of his own school, Hama's Dance Center, in Glendale. It is the style of Hama, with roots in Luigi but representative of his own ideals, that is the underlying strength of Hama's Dance Center and *Jazz Dance L.A.*

A majority of dance studios in L.A. present hip hop and contemporary jazz dance. It's the training that leads to work in the resident film, television, and video industry. But Hama wanted a place for artistic jazz dance to be presented, a place where all dancers and choreographers of the same mind set could come together and, as Hama says, "share our lives through a fascinating art form - jazz dance." Hama enlisted the aid of two who shared the passion - dancer and film student Betty Newton and noted teacher-performer-choreographer Claude Thompson - to map out a performance of concert jazz dance. *Jazz Dance L.A '94* was staged in July of that year, with 14 choreographers and two guest dance companies contributing work. Among these were Phineas Newborn III, Doug Caldwell, Marguerite Derricks, and Terry Best - many choreographers known more for their commercial work. It gave them the chance to explore avenues in jazz dance that were not possible in commercial work.

The concert has grown markedly in three years, with an audience that nears 1,000. It is comprised mostly of dancers and people from the business, but Betty Newton, co-producer and contributing choreographer, feels that the time is right to attract ticket buyers from the general population. She says that shows like *Stomp* and *Riverdance* have opened a door for jazz dance, which she feels is inherently entertaining. Therefore, *Jazz Dance L.A.* will be expanding their performance schedule from three shows to six shows over two weekends, and will be hiring a publicist to get the word out to the general community. This year's performances will be July 17-19 and 24-26 at 8 pm, and July 20 and 27 at 3 pm, at the Glendale Community College Auditorium, 1500 N. Verdugo Rd, Glendale, CA. Tickets are $15 in advance through Ticketmaster, or $20 at the door.

Returning choreographers include Terry Best, Debra Brockus, Reggie Brown, Christine Baltes, Doug Caldwell, Tracey Durbin, Marguerite Derricks, Billy Goodson, Denise Leitner, Keny Long, Phineas Newborn III, and Eartha Robinson. New for this year are Jason Myers, Tina Landin, Carlos Jones, and Yukari Ahoshi. Betty Newton will contribute a piece entitled "People in Search of a Life," set to a section of the *Clockers* soundtrack. It's theme is that "somewhere between hope and reality is joy." Hama will also debut a new piece with 8-12 dancers. This energetic piece, set in a jazzy, classic style, will open the concert.

Claude Thompson, whose dance pedigree includes Broadway shows, television, teaching and choreographing, as well as being a member of Alvin Ailey's original company, will return with a piece he debuted last year. It is a tribute to record producer Quincy Jones, called "On Q's Journey." For this, Thompson has collaborated on choreography with Keny Long, Ka-Ron Brown Lehman, and Eartha Robinson. It is a 30 minute piece that covers Jones's career from orchestrating jazz bands to his latest successes with scoring movie soundtracks. The piece utilizes many styles of jazz - blues, boogie, Latin, and classic. But Thompson stresses that this is more like a theatre piece, as it is performed with a full set and 18 dancers. For him, dance involves acting, and he demands a motive for all of his movement. "Dance has gotten too commercial, especially in L.A.," he says, and "On Q's Journey" is his effort to bring an artistic approach to dance back to this city.

As *Jazz Dance L.A.* grows, Hama sees his ultimate goal looming in the distance. A Broadway show consisting of the spectrum of jazz dance, similar in approach to Fosse's *Dancin'*, is what he envisions. He wants more people to see the art of jazz dance, and to learn to find their own personal expression through the medium. For him personally, jazz dance is a classic form, and he sticks to it religiously. It's what he teaches, and he does not change to appease the commercial trends. At Hama's Dance Center, if a student does not like his style, Hama encourages them to seek out others, even if it means going to another studio. "Jazz is versatile, everyone can bring out a different style. I go in my own style. It is not suitable for everybody, but some will see it and like it. I am myself."

But the respect Hama has for jazz dance and the vision of others is visible in *Jazz Dance L.A.*, where he regularly invites a multitude of jazz dance choreographers to share their particular expressions of jazz dance. Or, in Hama's words, "to share the passion" of jazz dance.

12
RHYTHM RE-INVENTED

STOMP, Bring in 'da Noise Bring in 'da Funk,
Jam on the Groove

Reprinted from *Dancer* with permission, Copyright August 1997

Rhythm is an integral component of life, starting with the rising and setting of the sun, the changing of the seasons, the cycles of our bodies. It is in our nature as human beings to recognize and respond to rhythm. When events happen, are experienced, and at a later time recur, they are recognized as familiar. We develop a sense of acceptance and safety in our lives, understanding our world due to having previously experienced some aspect of it. Then, by having a secure home base to return to, forays into the unknown are not so frightening.

This concept of rhythm and a recurring place is also the basis of jazz. A rhythm, whether a percussive beat or in the form of a melody, is stated. Soon the participants are delving off in improvisations, only to return and restate the original phrase. Another aspect of rhythm is its infectious quality, causing listeners to react with simple toe tapping or full body movement. But the point is that we all feel it. Rhythm is a basic human concept that cuts across all cultures.

From time to time in our 20th century society, rhythm has emerged in music and dance movement in various forms. Jazz and the Charleston replaced tin pan alley and stiff ballroom dances. Rock and roll brought a simpler beat back after the complicated syncopations of be bop jazz. And in the '70s, disco and funk surged in popularity after nearly a decade of experimentation and the dissolution of the rock beat. Recently, after a stale music and theatre scene and an increasingly technological and non-physical lifestyle has decimated our appreciation of rhythm, new forms of rhythmic expression are emerging. Due to

55

their natural appeal, they are finding widespread acceptance by an audience who may feel that they are experiencing something new.

Three shows that are now playing to packed and enthusiastic audiences are *STOMP*, *Bring in 'da Noise Bring in 'da Funk*, and *Jam on the Groove*. Although they each have a different approach, and rely on some tried and true tricks and comedic clichés, they can each claim rhythm as the core of their appeal. Audiences are packing theatres, reacting with wonder to the latest examples of human expression through rhythm. The beat utilized in these shows is not a jazz or swing beat, but a harsher attack more representative of our times. But the reintroduction and manipulation of rhythm is what dazzles the masses.

STOMP, the oldest and most successful of the three, has the least amount of traditional dance movement. The cast enchants the audience with the unexpected, finding clever catchy beats in everyday objects - brooms, cans, match boxes - even empty hoses. To command an audience simply with rhythm for two hours is nearly impossible, so *STOMP* is fleshed out with familiar comedy ideas, like the big guy vs. the little guy, and with audience participation. Without saying a word, the performers cajole the audience into sampling the thrill of the collective experience of rhythm by encouraging them to clap and join the performer's rhythms at the proper time. Simple, but wondrous. The audience loves it.

What most impressed me about *STOMP* was a section of hand clapping and body slapping by one performer. Complicated rhythms were pounded out with only the body as an instrument. Here, I thought, was the closest thing to seeing the roots of American jazz dancing. When African-Americans were brought to this country as slaves and were stripped of their musical instruments, they resorted to clapping, body slapping, and foot stomping as ways to provide rhythmic accompaniment. In *STOMP*, here was that very activity - delightfully performed and devilishly inventive. It was a stream of human feelings, expressed as rhythm, flowing from the performer's flesh like super conducted electricity.

Bring in 'da Noise Bring in 'da Funk carries the most serious tone of the three shows. It characterizes the rhythmic beat of African culture, and then depicts how that beat has been diluted, manipulated, and generally abused over the course of the last four centuries. Part history lesson and part theatrical extravaganza, *Bring in 'da Noise Bring in 'da Funk* at times imitates the use of props in *STOMP*, but primarily uses tap dancing as its main movement vocabulary. The underlying theme is that the beat is king, and it should not be manipulated and defiled by those who cannot appreciate it. The cast leads the audience on a tour of African-American dance history, including plantation dances, movie tap dancing, the migration of African-Americans to northern cities, and the futile attempts of minorities to just hail a cab - all illustrated with rhythmic tap dancing.

What the show promotes is a return to tap for the sake of evoking the beat. I saw a performance with Baakari Wilder as the lead, and in a group tap dance he and the cast advocate *hittin'*, or finding a groove and running with it. Its about letting tap be an expressive art, letting the feelings of the performer flow through the improvisations, rather than using the art in a lesser form. In this philosophy, tap dancing becomes almost a mystical experience, where the dancer, wrapped in rhythm, loses himself while evoking the beat.

But the very fact that *Bring in 'da Noise Bring in 'da Funk* is a theatrical show goes against the grain of this doctrine. While the cast is onstage *hittin'*, they are still performers, trying to evoke a response from the audience with their expertise. And the audience, at Broadway ticket prices, seems to react to those with the flashiest steps. *Bring in 'da Noise Bring in 'da Funk* wants to have it both ways, proclaiming the purity of the art, and then mass merchandising it at $70 a seat and $25 a t-shirt. In this locale, the art is still subservient to the demands of the marketplace, and therefore not as pure as it could be. Perhaps the ultimate *hittin'* takes place without an audience, in a back room with just the dancer and a floor - and the beat.

An opposite approach is used in *Jam on the Groove*, a hip hop dance musical. This show is clearly for audience entertainment, having sanitized the 1980s break dance movement of American ghettos and put it on display as exuberant, clean cut expression of the hip hop generation. Although they try to give scenarios to their dances (dice games and kung fu movies), the ideas are tame compared to the exposure of racism in *Bring in 'da Noise Bring in 'da Funk* As they proclaim, hip hop is about peace, love, unity...and having fun!

And fun is what they audience goes away with, mainly through the crew's incredible mastery of internalizing rhythmic isolation movement. Whether popping, locking, or boogalooing, the cast never fails to draw out the latent rhythmic aptitude of the audience. Add an extra heavy dose of acrobatic flair and head spins, and *Jam on the Groove* and its hard working, ever smiling dancers succeed in convincing us that rhythm is back with a vengeance.

The only drawback here is that every trick, no matter how thrilling, must then be topped by an even bigger trick. Since break dancing originated as a new urban folk dance, and as a means for young people to have confidence and develop stature within their community, it would be interesting to see how the company would approach a more serious topic closer to their home experience. This way, the theme, not the trick, would be the focus.

These three shows seem to be spearheading a trend in contemporary entertainment. Dance musicals do not have to be in the traditional Broadway style, and, similar to the case of the lindy and the birth of American theatrical jazz dancing in the 1940s, new urban folk dances are being utilized and expanded in order to create new avenues of expression. Rhythm, in its latest form, is again reaching mass audiences and communicating on a basic level. It sells because it touches people.

Combining the familiar vocabulary of popular dance movement, the theme of artistic expression, and the common sensual appeal of rhythm, these latest examples of shows based in the jazz dance tradition are making an immense impact on world cultures. And there lies the value of jazz dance as an artistic medium. We ALL can feel it. *STOMP*,

Bring in 'da Noise Bring in 'da Funk, and *Jam on the Groove* reach people of all ages and types. Which brings me to the conclusion of *STOMP*. After leading the audience in a chorus of finger snaps, the solo performer moved slowly upstage into the darkness To the accompaniment of nearly two thousand finger snaps, he faded away and uttered the only words in the show - "Can you feel it?" He disappeared...and the crowd snapped on.

13
SPECTRUM DANCE THEATER
COMMITTED TO DIVERSITY

Reprinted from *Dancer* with permission, Copyright September 1997

According to Webster's Dictionary, a "spectrum" is a series of radiations arranged in a regular order, or a continuous sequence of range. The word has also been associated with jazz dance, due to its range of styles and multi-cultural roots. Since 1982, a dedicated group of dancers has been building a successful jazz dance company in the Seattle area. They chose the name Spectrum Dance Theater to best describe their philosophy of presenting the sweeping range of jazz dance to the diverse cultural and socio-economic population of Seattle. Their strong belief in nurturing ties to the community, along with developing their artistic excellence, has now resulted in a firmly established regional jazz dance company that is poised to attain national prominence.

Spectrum Dance Theater's mission statement first and foremost is to bring " a greater realization of the value of dance." The company has been under the artistic direction of Dale Merrill since its inception, and

in a recent interview, he explained how the philosophy grew from the dance activities of the Madrona Dance Studio in center Seattle. "Our studio is located in a neighborhood where many people are not affluent, or can't afford to take dance class, or a lot of kids who can get into serious trouble...we always had that idea of trying to help people - give them activities that would really make them feel good about themselves.

Dance seemed to be the art form to do that...jazz dance seemed to be the perfect extension of that because of its multi-cultural aspect."

At the same time, Merrill and his company had backgrounds with ballet companies and serious concert dance. So they joined efforts to bring the highest quality of jazz dancing, a form of dance that draws from many different peoples, to the different peoples of their neighborhood and city. In the process they have provided the opportunity for local jazz dancers and choreographers to present their work, and brought recognition to Seattle by acquiring the works of internationally known choreographers.

The early efforts of the company focused on local jazz choreographers. People like Wade Madsen of the Cornish College of the Arts and Merrill himself. An American Jazz Tribute was produced by former American Dance Machine members Tinka Guttrick and Dannul Daily, Guy Caridi - director of the Savoy Swing Club, and Ray Bussey. A company member who has shown promise as a choreographer is Mark Kane. His *Of Passion, You Have Plenty*, set to an acid rock score, has garnered favorable reviews. Another local choreographer is Nancy Cranbourne, whose *Blue Plate Special*, set to songs by Frank Sinatra, was performed by Spectrum Dance Theater at the 1996 Jazz Dance World Congress at the Kennedy Center in Washington, DC. Thus the ties to the community and diversity in jazz dance styles presented.

But for the company to grow in stature and for the dancers to challenged artistically, Merrill decided to acquire works by national choreographers. Spectrum Dance Theater now performs pieces by Frank Chaves of River North Dance Company, Ann Reinking, Lynne Taylor-Corbett, Pattie Obey, Danny Buraczeski, and Claire Bataille of Hubbard Street Dance Chicago. With the addition in 1996 of *Waiting for the Sunrise* by Lar Lubovitch, the company can take pride in a repertory of jazz dance pieces by a list of name choreographers that easily rivals modern and classical dance companies with much larger budgets.

The company now has eleven dancers, including Merrill. Most have a strong basis in ballet technique, but did not identify with the characterizations of ballet performance. Of his dancers Merrill states "Most of them have danced with ballet companies, but ballet doesn't quite work for them." Personally, Merrill has "a hard time relating to how men and women relate to each other, or the way women are portrayed" in ballet. But they find that in jazz dance, the dancers are portraying real people, not "inanimate objects," and the expression is synonymous with how they feel. "And most of the women in our company are the same way. There is a strength and power, I think, to a woman in a jazz company that sometimes a ballet woman doesn't get to express."

As a company, the dancers take class in ballet and in jazz dance. Merrill teaches the jazz class, and he draws from a range of technique and stylistic approaches. After spending many years as an aspiring ballet dancer with the University of Utah, he began to look to jazz. His early

classes were with Roland Dupree, and in summer sessions with the Alvin Ailey American Dance Center in New York. But his real influence came in the form of an intensive three month workshop in the style and technique of Jack Cole.

Merrill says "I don't teach a Jack Cole class, because most people couldn't or wouldn't do that. But as a choreographer, there are parts of that that we use in our classes and in the pieces that we do."

Merrill's eclectic approach to jazz dance and basis in technique has enabled his dancers to perform a variety of jazz dance styles, and contribute to the company's mission of diversity. The stylistic range of the repertory includes lyrical, Broadway, modern, comic, swing, funk, and classic forms of jazz dance. Although they receive the NEA minimum when they are working, the dancers are employed part time through out the year. Most supplement their income by teaching or doing free lance work.

Merrill is particularly pleased with the acquisition of Lar

Lubovitch's *Waiting for the Sunrise*. Lubovitch releases only five works per year, so the selection of Spectrum Dance Theater places ranks it with companies of national prominence and high artistic merit. Although Lubovitch is not known as a jazz dance choreographer, Merrill feels that *Waiting for the Sunrise* qualifies as jazz dance due to its subject matter, and use of music by the 1950s duo of Les Paul and Mary Ford. The piece draws from the social dance movements of the '50s, and employs the use of isolation in movement. The folk aspect of the choreography, combined with the feel of the jazz related music, made *Waiting for the Sunrise* an excellent choice to add to the company's repertory.

Funding has come from some major corporations and arts councils, including Boeing Corporation, Microsoft Corporation, SAFECO Insurance, Bank of America, and Digital Equipment Corporation, although the levels of funding do not rival the amounts given to some of Seattle's larger classical companies. Merrill says that the company is on the brink of jumping to a higher category of funding, which will happen when their budget exceeds $350,000 per year. He cites SAFECO as notable for paying for new choreography, while some of the others prefer to fund arts education projects.

Which is fine with Merrill, as the company's mandate to retain its ties to its community and educate its audience has worked well in developing new audiences. Two projects have done well - *The American Way of Dance*, a 45 minute presentation showing the evolution of jazz dance; and the *Family Matinee Performance* - where Merrill introduces the audience to all aspects of the production of a dance piece and entertains an audience discussion following the performance. He also states that Spectrum is aided by Seattle's strong jazz music presence, and the awareness of the media and arts funders of the music style. The typical resistance and prejudice that most jazz dance companies meet is not a problem for the company.

Merrill's task for the future is to increase the amount of work weeks for the dancers, and that can only come from touring. He feels that Spectrum has "maxxed out" the opportunities for performances in the Seattle area, so the road is the place to add more work. The company has retained two management agencies to book tours, and is looking to the opportunities given by Gus Giordano's Jazz Dance World Congresses to develop a higher profile. In August, 1997, the company will travel to Weisbaden, Germany, to perform with the Congress and establish European ties. After that, its back to Seattle for their annual fall concert from September 19 - 21. In addition to *Waiting for the Sunrise, An American Tribute*, and *Of Passion, You Have Plenty*, the company will present the Northwest premiere of Danny Buraczeski's *Fuerza Viva*, about the influence of Latino and Hispanic cultures on jazz dance and music. The piece goes well with the stated mission of Spectrum Dance Theater - to bring a greater realization of the value of dance by presenting American Contemporary dance to a diverse audience. If artistic director Dale Merrill has his way, Spectrum Dance Theater's audience will soon surpass its regional borders and swell to national, if not international, proportions.

14
DECIDEDLY JAZZ DANCEWORKS

Reprinted from *Dancer* with permission, Copyright October 1997

Since jazz dance evolved on our continent, we Americans tend to be possessive and take credit for being the leaders and innovators in the field. We sometimes think of jazz dance as being uniquely American,

 and for that reason, we have special rights to the form. But there is a tremendous amount of interest in jazz dance by dancers from other countries. One company in particular, Decidedly Jazz Danceworks of Calgary, Alberta, is on the forefront of concert jazz dance, and is an entity from which many American jazz dancers can take a few lessons.

The name - Decidedly Jazz Danceworks - says it all. The company, led by co-founders Vicki Adams Willis, Michele Moss, and Hannah Stilwell, rejects the notion of non-artistry normally appended to jazz dance and takes pride in choosing the swinging rhythms of jazz music and its resultant movement idiom as fuel for their choreographic fires. At the Jazzart Technique and Choreography Workshop, held at Western Kentucky University in July, I was able to speak with Vicki Adams Willis and Michele Moss at length about the surging success of their company, and their upcoming October season in Calgary.

Willis was teaching jazz dance at the University of Calgary in the late 1970s and early 1980s, and in 1984, two of her students, Moss and Stilwell, approached her with the idea of forming a jazz dance company. Willis agreed, and she became the primary choreographer for a four person company. The dancers were "adamant about jazz being jazz," and

67

the new company's philosophy, according to Willis was "to create an awareness of and encourage a respect for the traditional spirit and integrity of jazz." Moss backed up this credo by saying " the spirit of jazz - that is something very important to us. Not archival - but something that honors the history and ancestry, but keeps moving to the future and is innovative." By staying true to their philosophy and their dream, in just 13 years the company has grown to eight dancers and can boast a $1.4 million dollar budget. The company has performed internationally, and the DJD school has an enrollment of 700 students.

At first, the dancers had to literally chart their own course, choreographically and as a developing company. There weren't obvious role models for jazz dance companies, and Moss said that "the modern dance aesthetic was strong, because we were trying to make 'concert work.'" They had to research jazz dance movements, and find out where they came from and what they meant. This was the beginning of a strong interest in the African heritage of jazz dance rhythms and movements. And the company began to open up to many new influences - African, Afro-Cuban, Latin, tap, East Indian, and flamenco.

Although they still teach some classes for the university, the directors opened their own school and continued building the

company. Help from Canadian funding agencies was not forthcoming. Moss said "for the longest time we were not even considered. There was the dance division - which included ballet and modern. Then there was folk dance and everything else." This lack of understanding by funding agencies, common to most jazz dance companies, plagued DJD until about two years ago, when a category was created to accommodate jazz dance.

But the natural appeal of jazz dance, and DJD's innovative qualities has led to an unprecedented growth in audience attendance. The company has two seasons each year in Calgary, and in October 1996 drew over 5,000 people in five performances. The company has toured throughout Alberta, British Columbia, the Maritimes, Ottawa, and has been invited to the Montreal Jazz Festival and the World Jazz Dance Congresses in Chicago and Japan. At the 1994 Congress, the Chicago press called DJD "the highlight of the festival."

Another reason for the company's rapid growth is the fact that DJD has made it a priority to educate the audiences of Canada about jazz dance and jazz music. To get people to accept you on your terms, they first must know where you are coming from. The directors have spent many hours enlightening the media, funding agencies, school systems, and even senior citizens. They tour three educational performances - *Live and in Sync* for elementary schools, *Random Leaps of Faith* for junior and senior high schools, and *Swingtime* for senior citizens.

Live music is used in one of the Calgary seasons each year. This is expensive, but pays off in the quality of the performance and the inspiration to dancers and choreographers from the musicians, and helps to put DJD a notch higher than companies who only use taped music. It also gives the choreographers another tool in developing their pieces. DJD has commissioned scores for their performances from the likes of Mark Murphy, Big Miller, Tommy Banks, P.J. Berry, and Diane Miller. A recent performance, *Rhythm Addiction*, required an intricate piece of music that segued from one rhythm style to another. Only by working hand in hand with the musicians could the proper music be developed. Eventually the original score was produced on a CD, and the company uses it as a fundraiser.

Willis said that the company's rep is primarily based in swing dance, but experimentation has led them into many new areas. About five years ago the company sought out new choreographers to widen the company's vision. After looking in many areas and "many trips to New York," the company has added pieces by Billy Siegenfeld and Montreal's Michael Montanaro. They have also ventured into tap dance, and brought in tap master Buster Brown and Manhattan Tap's Heather Cornell for *No Small Feets* in 1992 and 1993. Montanaro devised an evening performance based in film noir for *Stolen Moments* in 1995.

69

The company does not follow a particular jazz technique, but is satisfied to operate within the eclectic spectrum of jazz dance influences. "It's always been a beg-borrow kind of style, in terms of folk music and dance" said Moss, and the training of the dancers reflects that varied background. Ballet class is given three time per week, and the directors will also give weekly classes based on their own direction in jazz dance. Tap has become popular in recent years, and the company also receives classes in African, modern, Afro-Cuban, and other styles. They are paid a living wage, but many choose to augment their salaries through teaching. The company suffers the same problem shared by many regional companies, that of losing dancers to the bigger cities, companies, and paychecks. Which is fine with the directors, as they feel that if the dancer is happiest in a bigger environment, then they belong there.

But Moss said that many dancers, after experiencing the pace and pressure of top dance companies, return to Calgary and DJD to work in jazz dance in a friendlier atmosphere. They come back for the work, and for the chance to have "a life." The directors are quite content with the scope of their operation, and are proud of establishing a system where they can work in their chosen field, at the pace they would like to, and still have time to go home and have a family and a life other than dance. The company could gain more notoriety by pursuing a heavy touring schedule, but the directors are happy just to take opportunities as they come about. To them, having time to work in the studio and present new work to their Calgary audience is the primary objective, and has brought them the most satisfaction in terms of choreographic expression and audience acceptance. Their lives are about exploring the artistic application of jazz dance, not the dog eat dog world of dance company performing and politics. Obviously, with a current operating budget of $1.4 million dollars, a large school, and drawing the largest audience of any performing group on Calgary (a city of 800,000), their devotion to the roots of jazz dance and their unwavering belief in their vision has paid off well.

Decidedly Jazz Danceworks will present their latest work in jazz dance with *Optic Verve*, an evening of premieres choreographed by some of North America's most dazzling dance makers, from October 21-26 at the Max Bell Theatre of the Calgary Centre for the Performing Arts. Choreographers include Billy Siegenfeld (who was just awarded this year's Ruth Page Award as best choreographer in Chicago), Katherine Kramer, Michael Montanaro, Jeannie Hill of the Jump Rhythm Jazz Project, and DJD directors Hannah Stilwell and Michele Moss. The company will show jazz dance that ranges from hot tap solos to smooth and languid ensemble work.

Hopefully the company will be enticed to travel south at some point so we Americans can see how jazz dance heats up the cold winters of Canada. The company's remarkable statistics prove that they are doing something right, and directors Willis, Moss, and Stilwell obviously can teach us a thing or two about our own game. Here's hoping that Calgary and Canada can part with their unique dance company, and that a tour of the "homeland" will happen soon.

15
JAZZ DANCE AMBASSADORS
TEACHERS ON THE FRONTLINE

Reprinted from *Dancer* with permission, Copyright January 1998

Jazz Dance is at a crossroad. If one takes a look back at our recent history, it is evident that intervening factors of changes in music, society, and technology are again forcing jazz dance to adapt and conform to a new set of parameters. The playing field keeps changing and there are many dancers and teachers, unhappy with the new vision of jazz dance, who are applying creative ways of keeping jazz dance within their prescribed direction.

At the Jazzart Jazz Dance Technique and Choreography Workshop held in July 1997 at Western Kentucky University, many teachers who fight the battle for jazz dance integrity convened for a rap session on the future of teaching and choreographing as jazz dance artists. Among the 25 teachers participating in the workshop were Lori Maxwell of Calgary, Alberta; Isabelle Cook of Veradale, Washington; Erja Fischer of Narragansett, Rhode Island; Linda Dahlstrom of Panama; Judy Woodruff of Johnson City, Tennessee; Christine Hounsell of Rochester, New Hampshire; Deb Belue of Nashville, Tennessee; Cynthia Hamilton of Spokane, Washington; Gail Benedict of Louisville, Kentucky; and Beverly Veenker of Bowling Green, Kentucky.

The first item of discussion was the changes in jazz dance classes and education in the last 30 years. In a move that is symptomatic of much of our society, jazz dance education has been drifting away from more regimented schools and syllabi under the directorship of a well known jazz dance innovator, to a more mobile and varying direction of study. In the 1950s and 60s, most jazz dance education took place in the major cities of New York, Chicago, and Los Angeles. Within these cities you would find schools under the directorship of jazz pioneers like

Matt Mattox, Luigi, Gus Giordano, and Eugene Loring. These teachers were always available for class, and they had a strict system of technique exercises that was the foundation for their movement style and jazz dance personality. But as times changed, Mattox left for Europe, Loring's school closed, and Luigi was the victim of spiraling rents in NYC, forcing him to move constantly. The Giordano Dance Center is the only of these major jazz dance training schools still in existence in its original format. Beverly Veenker, associate professor of dance at Western Kentucky University, remembers that "years ago, each substantial teacher had a school, and you could choose who you would study with. Then the schools closed, and you had to hop around. Then you couldn't find a teacher with whom you could study for a long time."

Gail Benedict, a former Fosse assistant, star of many Broadway shows and now a teacher for the Youth Performing Arts School in Louisville, KY, noted some of the after effects of this evolution. "Proteges of these people started to teach, but they were just giving class, they really weren't teaching the technique - how to do it. They just basically came in and showed up. You went to watch the person dance, and hopefully learn by copying them. They didn't teach you how or what you were doing. That was because there was a lot of money to be made. Whoever was hot or got to choreograph a new show was teaching. The classes were packed, and there was never any limit to the number."

When asked about what jazz dance techniques they now teach, most agreed that they teach an amalgam of many jazz and non-jazz techniques. Many use exercises from the Lester Horton modern dance technique as a warm up, and then use isolation exercises from Mattox or Charles Kelley. Lynn Simonson was mentioned for her technique, and praised for still running a school and teaching technique in NYC according to the older model of jazz dance instruction. One thing they were in agreement on, was that there is a lack of jazz dance instructional material, in the form of books and videos, and that training schools of a short amount of time were not successful in instilling a deeper grasp and understanding of technique. To really master jazz dance technique, you need to have regular exposure to knowledgeable instructors with class sizes that encourage personal contact.

Another point that irked many of the teachers was having new students approach their schools and classes with a pre-conceived notion as to what they wanted to learn in a jazz class. Television and MTV are the culprits, they say, in transmitting an overwhelming image of a rough edged, street dance look. Most agreed that the look on videos is one where a person should appear to have no training, or to be a natural. When young dancers come to a school with this role model in mind, they can soon be put off by a class that teaches body control through a set system of exercises. These dancers see the fun and joy of dance, but do not realize the work that goes into it. So, the lack of suitable role models for technique oriented jazz dance is a stumbling point in teachers being able to run their classes as they wish.

This mention of MTV moved the conversation in a related area - the lack of work for dancers. Gail Benedict was vocal about the method of hiring and paying dancers for music videos. "There are great artists - like Michael Jackson, "she said, "but as a sustainable lifestyle, with video dancers not receiving residuals, it does not promote the job of a dancer."

When pressed for ways to promote jazz dance and work for jazz dancers, all agreed that nothing will change without dedicated people, passionate about jazz dance, who are willing to work at a grass roots level to educate the public and the media. The biggest problem is the lack of understanding of jazz dance by funders, media people, and the general public. When many of the teachers have tried to apply for funding as a jazz dance company or performance, funding agencies have denied their requests on the basis that jazz dance is not an art. Or, they find it hard to be noticed when there isn't even a dance category for jazz. Newspaper editors often allocate their dance coverage to ballet and modern dance companies, and for some reason have the terrible habit of covering a performance after the fact rather than before it. And as for the general public, with the massive exposure of videos defining the image of jazz dance, the chance to present a different image of jazz dancing is not forthcoming.

The tough question to be answered was: how can these restricting parameters be changed or circumvented, allowing a more accurate image of jazz dance to be portrayed? All agreed that without people passionate about jazz dance, willing to become volunteer jazz dance ambassadors, jazz dance will be swept into a rapidly escalating tide of commercialism. On the aspect of technique, all felt that they ran smaller schools with an emphasis on technique, rather than large enrollment schools that cater to those just wanting to have fun. Erja Fischer said that she closed a large school, and re-opened in a smaller format so that she could have less overhead and teach the way she wanted. Lori Maxwell, speaking of the Decidedly Jazz Danceworks school in Canada, said that artistic director Vicki Willis is trying to preserve the traditions of jazz - teaching specific exercises from specific techniques. Their school has a library of books and videos available to all, and all of the teachers are audited on a regular basis. Linda Dahlstrom felt that ..."in Latin America and Mexico, commercialism is seen as better. We lose students, but we firmly believe in the way we are doing it."

Cynthia Hamilton said that in Spokane, Washington, about 30 dance schools have banded together in a local alliance to promote dance as an art form in local presentations and for National Dance Week. She also felt that it was important to get acquainted with your local newspaper editor. "Take them out for coffee or lunch, get to know them and let them know you." It is unpaid volunteer work, but it the work needed to be done to improve the conditions for jazz dance.

As for the general public, their viewpoints will only be enlightened by a steady and consistent diet of jazz dance performances, lectures, and educational material. First, get your students out to see live performances. Use the purchasing power of a large group from your studio to negotiate a group rate. Presenters usually have empty seats, so the larger your group, then better rate you can ask for. But the teacher has to be the one to insist that the student attend. Without this enforcement, live performances will dwindle, and so will jobs for dancers. Also mentioned was approaching your local presenter with a list of possible jazz dance companies to hire. Make copies of jazz dance company profiles from past editions of this column, or print them off of the *Jazz Dance Homepage* web site. Bring these companies to the attention of presenters, and volunteer to sell tickets on a group sale basis. And when a company does come to your city, contact the company manager and arrange for a master class at your studio with someone who will be performing. It gives you notoriety, and provides extra incentive for your students.

Within your studio, have a section with jazz dance books and videos available to your students on a check out basis. Encourage them to look at the dances, and then discuss them in class. Set up a Saturday video showing in your studio, maybe after the last class or rehearsal, so that if even for a half hour, the teacher has the chance to bring jazz dance history and choreography to the attention of a group of dancers. A good suggestion was to have your dancers watch a particular jazz dance, and then try to recreate some of the choreography in class.

The solutions suggested by this band of jazz dance ambassadors are not hard to implement. In fact, most are relatively simple. But they require dedication and commitment, and implementation over the long term. They are not something to be taken up at a whim. For those who really are passionate about jazz dance, they will be a joy to execute. Jazz dance teachers not only love jazz dance, but they love to teach, to educate, to bring the joy of jazz dance to others the way it was given to them. A common theme expressed was that, even though today's kids are inundated with commercial music, they still respond to jazz and swing when given the chance. There is a pleasure in jazz music and dance, whether done for a living or just for the experience. And there is the connection to people that only a teacher can achieve.

Jazz dance needs ambassadors to spread the philosophy of technique and expression, and that the feeling of jazz dance cannot be usurped by commercialism. It needs people willing to fight the battle on the front lines, in the local dance studios and the small theatres as well as the major performing arts venues and mass media. It needs the person who is willing to stand up for a philosophy. The essence of the discussion was captured by Lori Maxwell, who said "It all depends on who is the guru of the school. If there is a passion that you exude, people will come."

16
JAZZ DANCE MASTER – BILLY SIEGENFELD

Reprinted from *Dancer* with permission, Copyright February 1998

Like modern dance, the creation of theatrical jazz dancing was based on the unique visions of innovators with a fresh, well articulated point of view. Whether Graham, Humphrey, and Weidman; or Cole, Mattox, Luigi, Robbins, and Fosse - all formulated personal visions and dared to take time to develop and expand upon their instinctual feelings on dance. As I mentioned in my last column, the world of jazz dancing in recent years has moved towards a mish-mosh of styles and techniques, forsaking the methods of these visionaries. But within the great morass of American jazz dance, a new innovator is emerging - someone with a fresh, well articulated vision like the great masters of years past. That newly acknowledged master of jazz dance is Billy Siegenfeld, professor of dance at Northwestern University and artistic director of the Jump Rhythm Jazz Project.

Siegenfeld is no stranger to those in the know of jazz dance. He has choreographed for Joffrey II, Ballet Pacifica, Decidedly Jazz Danceworks, JazzCool (a company from the Netherlands), as well as received the Golden Leo Award for Outstanding Choreography at the 1994 Jazz Dance World Congress. This past September he was honored with the best choreography award from the Chicago Dance Coalition, and he has received three grants from the NEA. But this master, known everywhere simply as Billy, has up to now been mainly involved in choreography for other companies, or for his Jump Rhythm Jazz Project consisting of him and associate director Jeannie Hill. I was able

to speak with Billy prior to one of his master classes at NY's Broadway Dance Center, and I asked him about his vision of jazz dance, and his plans for a full fledged JRJP company.

"The Jump Rhythm Jazz Technique," he explained, "honors and extends the tradition of jazz dancing featured in the performances of artists like Astaire, the Nicholas Brothers, Fosse, Haney, and Sammy Davis, Jr. The chief aim of the technique is to communicate to dancers the joy of moving in a musically expressive way - of being able to produce movement that makes visible the syncopated, dynamically rich rhythms of swinging jazz, the blues, and Latin jazz. The technique physically amplifies accents in the body by using jazz dynamics, and is performed in rhythmic phrases that combine both downbeat and off beat accents. The goal is total body rhythm making." He stated that, in his opinion, "for dancing to be considered jazz dancing it must incorporate the essential element of swing, and that for dance to swing, it must be performed to the great music of jazz composers like Ellington, Monk, Brown, and others."

Billy's technique and style has been best represented in performances by himself and Hill as the JRJP. Although he has enjoyed choreographing for other companies and is grateful for the opportunity to do so, like most choreographers with a well defined vision and limited time the result onstage does not match the vision in the head. On his work for other companies Billy said "If they have not been trained in both the point of view and the neuromuscular circuitry that you already have, because its your own, then no amount of sincerity, ecstasy, ambition, and good heart is going to take what's in your brain and put it out there on the stage... I realized that what I had to do was what all the people who have had companies, created the companies for. They created them to actually train a group of people to talk their talk, in the way they talk."

Siegenfeld has now sufficiently matured as an artist to feel confident in setting his point of view on a newly formed company of jazz dancers. Once he felt that he had an actual point of view to explore, Billy set out on an experiment. He began working with eight dancers in

August, and has judged the initial stage of this experiment to be a success. Their first showing was for Dance Chicago in October 1997, dancing *Gettin' To It*, the third section of a suite of songs to the music of bassist Christian McBride. (*Gettin' To It* was first sketched in a choreography workshop at the 1997 Jazzart Technique and Choreography Workshop.) What was noted in the dancing and choreography was a rhythmic unison that had never been seen before in his work. This clarity of dancing, in both technique and expression, was what Billy had been looking for. "I was sitting there in the dark - lo and behold - gratified! I have not had that feeling in my 27 years of dancing."

Billy elaborated on the methods utilized to get the vision in his head onto the stage. His first action was to insist on three company classes per week, in order to have dancers well versed in the dynamic physical and musical intricacies of the Jump Rhythm Jazz Technique. Unlike many of today's jazz companies, but like the masters of the past, he trained his dancers in a formal technique that is derived from the needs of his choreography. Second, he decided that it was finally time for him to get down to business, and not settle for less than the vision in his head. "Part of the experience was finding out how to do this more rigorous disciplining of eight other human beings who by definition don't want to do what you want to do...how to do that without having to pass into that archaic philosophy that dictated the way companies functioned in the old days." Without resorting to the abusive tactics of other choreographers, Billy set up what he called a "benign autocracy," meaning that, although he would not yell at dancers, he would definitely be the final authority, and it would be entirely acceptable for him to say "No, that's not right."

In terms of expression, Billy urged his dancers to redefine how they approached dancing in general. He feels that much of today's technically oriented dancing produces dancers who only respond to movement on a visual level, and not on an emotional level. With the accentuation on maximum flexibility and more distorted visual appeal in each movement, classes today reinforce the fallacy that audiences must be in awe of performers, rather than feel a kinship with them. "Awe," Billy said, "is based on a sense of inferiority. They [the audience] are saying I can't do that." This produces a chasm between spectator and performer, and the awe factor dissipates after a few minutes, leaving the spectator hungry for even greater tricks.

"Today's dance," he feels, "with its emphasis on higher and more, has lost its connection to the ground, and therefore to rhythm. Even in ballet, there is a rhythm in the proper execution of steps." He is elated that his dancers are willing to understand that "this rhythmic gig I am doing is actually a rhythmic *emotional* gig. Because that's what rhythm is. Rhythm is always an interiorly felt sensation. Yeah, you beat against the floor, but its an energy thing, not a shape thing...its a felt sensation, whose outward manifestation is a shape." Since rhythm is a universal human emotion, and the movements and personalities he chooses are derivative of everyday life, Billy strives for a style of jazz dance that the audience can identity with. As with Astaire and other great masters, Billy wants to connect with audiences on their level, not be distanced from them.

Whether Billy's point of view will be adopted by the mainstream of jazz dancing remains to be seen. It is true, however, that he has become increasingly in demand as a choreographer and teacher in recent years, and people all over the world have been joyously re-introduced to the classic rhythms of jazz dance through his efforts. Billy Siegenfeld has used the components of the classic performances of jazz dancing as the basis of his Jump Rhythm Jazz Technique, successfully inventing the first genuine jazz dance technique in forty years. With any luck, his use of the methods of the masters of jazz and modern dance in creating a company will spread the Jump Rhythm credo of rhythm and expression, allowing dancers and spectators worldwide to rediscover their inherent wellspring of dance emotions.

17
MAKING A DIFFERENCE –
MARCUS ALFORD AND ANNIE DAY

Reprinted from *Dancer* with permission, Copyright March 1998

In my January column, I wrote about being an ambassador for jazz dance by taking up the necessary but often overlooked task of advocacy. Teachers of jazz dance are making a difference in the

Marcus R. Alford

perception of our art by taking the time to bring the artistic aspect of jazz dance to the public. On a larger scale, there are many who promote jazz dance by becoming organizers as well as dancers and choreographers. Those who realize this transition find that they can make their own breaks and opportunities, and exert a profound influence on the character of jazz dance. A prime example of this type of ambassador is the husband and wife team of Marcus Alford and Annie Day.

Dance studios, a performance company, jazz festivals, educational materials, freelance choreographers - Marcus Alford and Annie Day have been instrumental in carrying the banner for jazz dance in all forms. They co-direct one of the nation's largest dance schools, Dancecentre South, in Atlanta, Georgia, and Marcus is the artistic director of Jazz Dance Theatre South, a professional touring jazz dance company. In addition to their heavy schedule of appearances as choreographers and teachers for national conventions and teaching organizations, Marcus has found time to write a textbook on jazz dance, *Jazz Danceology - The Teaching and Choreographing of Jazz Dance*, and direct

Jazz on Tap, the metro Atlanta Jazz and Tap Dance Festival.

You would think that with such a plate full of activity, Marcus and Annie would be either exhausted, burned out, or both. I witnessed the pair giving master classes for the Tennessee chapter of the Dance Masters of America in November and, quite to the contrary, found them to be animated, vivacious, and concerned about their students - with Marcus being in possession of a comic wit worthy of *Saturday Night Live*. In between teaching classes and then rushing to judge the competition performance, the duo were able to offer a glimpse of the upcoming 12th annual *Jazz on Tap* festival, this year to be held on March 13 and 14 at the Joe Mack Wilson Student Center Theatre, Southern Polytechnic University, in Marietta, Georgia.

Jazz on Tap is the south's primary avenue for exposure to all forms of jazz dance for the concert stage. This year's festival will bring 34 companies and in excess of 600 dancers, from dance school to professional, to show choreography and experience classes. Three performances are given to a total audience of nearly 1500. In terms of giving exposure to a high quality of jazz dance, *Jazz on Tap* is one of the premier jazz dance festivals in the country.

Jazz on Tap provides benefits to jazz dance on many levels. Even though the focus of the weekend is the performance opportunities given to young dancers, the festival in addition features master classes in jazz dance. By bringing together so many who appreciate jazz dance, it is also a valuable chance for teachers and choreographers to network and be inspired by the work of others. And it is a way for professional jazz companies to get the reviews and media stories that they need when proving stability and worth for funding agencies.

A particular aspect of Jazz on Tap that Annie takes pride in is the chance for young dancers to see artistic jazz dance for the first time.

Some of the companies and dancers, she noted, practice only recital or competition choreography. The festival is their awakening to jazz dance as an artistic expression. Annie sees this broadening exposure as a needed element of the total education of the jazz dancer and the general public.

When asked why he directs such a massive undertaking, Marcus quipped "Well, it's definitely not the money!" With a more reflective tone, he continued "There are three reasons. First, it's a sounding board for teachers, choreographers, and students. Second, it came out of a frustration with not enough organizations around the country with jazz and tap coming together - the two go hand in hand. We need that. Third - it is something we all love. It was put in my heart by Gus Giordano, the way it used to be. This is the chance to share - it's not a competition, although we do have competition numbers. But it's a concert environment."

Although the duo enjoy much notoriety because of *Jazz on Tap*, the idea to keep in mind is that the festival and its opportunities exist due to the devotion that Marcus and Annie have to jazz dance. Without their fortitude and backing and willingness to volunteer for their art, hundreds of dancers would not experience growth in their dance education, and audiences would not come to enjoy the sedate and sizzling moods of jazz dance. Their hard work, perseverance, and desire to plant the seeds of jazz dance appreciation has affected the course of many lives and the evolution of our art form. *Jazz on Tap* is the kind of venue that jazz dance desperately needs. Marcus Alford and Annie Day are jazz dance ambassadors of a distinguished level - artists who also use their skills as promoters to give jazz dance the visibility and credibility it rightfully deserves.

Jazz on Tap will be presented at the Joe Mack Wilson Student Center Theatre, Southern Polytechnic University, in Marietta, Georgia, on Friday, March 13 at 7:30 pm and Saturday, March 14 at 1:00pm and 7:30 pm. Tickets are $9 for adults, and $6 for seniors, students, and children under 12. For more information, call 770.516.7229.

18
GRACIELA DANIELE AND THE
NEED FOR JAZZ DANCE TECHNIQUE – PART 1

Reprinted from *Dancer* with permission, Copyright April 1998

In the musical theatre, the accomplished director/choreographer has diminished in importance since the deaths of Bob Fosse, Michael Bennett, and Gower Champion. These giants have been replaced by some newcomers who have made their mark on Broadway, but have not yet achieved the notoriety of a Bob Fosse or Jerome Robbins. One person, although not a newcomer to the Broadway tradition, has been steadily contributing to the legacy of dance in the musical theatre. Graciela Daniele was born in Argentina, danced professionally in France, and made a career out of dancing, choreographing, and directing on Broadway. She represents the best of American musical theatre dance. After her start as a classical ballet dancer, Ms. Daniele studied the techniques of Jack Cole and Matt Mattox, and danced with Fosse, Bennett, and others, before beginning a career in creating musicals. Her most recent triumph is the acclaimed staging in the Broadway production of *Ragtime*. This column, the first of two parts, includes edited responses to questions on jazz dance technique answered by Ms. Daniele during a rehearsal break from *Ragtime*.

Q. What is your dance background, and how did you get started in musical theatre?

I am from Argentina, where I studied ballet from an early age. I went to Paris at the age of 16 to dance in a ballet company. While I was in Paris, I saw a production of *West Side Story*, and it changed my life. At that time, at the age of 23 (1963), I decided to come to New York to study musical theatre. Before I came to New York, I asked around who are the best teachers to in New York to work with, and everybody said Matt Mattox. So I went to Matt's school. I owe him so much, but most of all for the knowledge that jazz is just not flinging your arms around and doing big tricks, that it was a very serious technique. And a very complete one. But he was fascinating - when I went to professional class and it used to be in the evening, and they would go instead of for an hour and a half, it would be for like three hours. You would be bleeding and sweating, and you wouldn't be stopping because it was such a high.

[Note: Matt Mattox is a jazz teacher who developed a set of technique exercises based in the style and movements of jazz dance pioneer Jack Cole. Mattox taught this technique in New York from 1955 to 1970.]

Q. What qualities do you look for in dancers when you are auditioning?

It all depends on the piece that I am doing. I don't have necessarily the "ideal" professional dancer, because I believe that we have to serve the piece, and what the piece needs - the style of the piece - is what I'm looking for in that particular show. I'm going to be rather cruel and say that I expect technique. I mean, without technique, what are you doing here? So technique is secondary to me because it has to be there. That's your language, you have to speak your language. What I look for is that kind of personality that takes them away from the chorus line. So I look for individuals. I look for actually the acting ability into the jazz. I think that's partially true what Matt had, and actually what Jack had. Jack Cole, you know, was the creator of it all.

Q. The techniques of Cole and Mattox are not readily accessible to young dancers today. Do today's dancers know these techniques, and where can they find them?

I don't think that it is the kids, so much. First of all, you have to teach the technique. You know the kids won't know the techniques, you have to have people who are teaching that technique. But I have to say, on the other hand, that there are two sides to it. I believe that everything is about supply and demand. In my time, when I came into it, dance was of that quality on the stage...That's what the dance was about. And therefore, we were created, we were built to supply that. It's not the kids. It's not even the choreographers. It's the material. That [Cole style dancing] is not what's on the stage right now. So what do you do? I would still advise the young kids to learn the technique [Cole/Mattox], because the technique will help them in everything they do. And that is because it is a technique that is just not American. It's just not based on American ethnic dance. There is no such thing as American ethnic dance, except square dancing. It's based on so many other cultures that Jack pulled from. The African, the Oriental - and he mixed it in his own fabulous language. Which is the language that taught Fosse and taught Robbins. There wouldn't be any Fosse or Robbins without Jack Cole. You know my love for them. But he was the creator. He was the one who created the technique. So I think that it is very important to learn the technique, because it teaches you so many other styles of dance...if you know the technique, you can do everything. The thing about the technique [Cole's] was that it gave you the ability to do any kind of style - because everything is derivative of that technique. All the styles that came after - the Robbins', everybody - we are all derivatives of that technique. You could satisfy any of the other styles by knowing that basis. Like, if you know one Roman language, it's easier to learn the others.

Q. You mentioned adding acting to the technique. How does a dancer do that, and what does it add to the performance?

It's an inner understanding of what you are doing and how you do it that brings a freedom to forget about technique because technique is there. And that's something we don't have too much of now - unfortunately. Technique has to be there automatically, so you can put it behind you, so that the emotion, freedom, and projection can come through. I used to love that about Chita [Rivera]. I looked at this woman, and when she started dancing, you didn't think about the technique because there was such a great freedom in her, you know. When you looked at her and she did her step, a back attitude, that step looked absolutely free but it took a long time for her to know where her center was and how far she could go. That's technique, and she put the technique behind because it was there already and then she could perform, she could act - that's what I look for in dancers. When you have that self discipline when the technique doesn't show so that you forget about the steps. But to bring that feeling, that emotion out, you have to start with technique first. And that takes a long, long time.

**In May - part 2 of an interview with Graciela Daniele - more on her work with Jack Cole, Bob Fosse, why people should dance, lack of discipline in today's dance, and what she "hates" about American culture.

19
GRACIELA DANIELE AND THE
NEED FOR JAZZ DANCE TECHNIQUE – PART 2

Reprinted from *Dancer* with permission, Copyright May 1998

Graciela Daniele was born in Argentina, danced professionally in France, and made a career out of dancing, choreographing, and directing on Broadway. She represents the best of American musical theatre dance. After her start as a classical ballet dancer, Ms. Daniele studied the techniques of Jack Cole and Matt Mattox, and danced with Fosse, Bennett, and others, before beginning a career in creating musicals. Her most recent triumph is the acclaimed staging in the Broadway production of Ragtime. This column, the second of two parts, includes edited responses to questions on jazz dance technique answered by Ms. Daniele during a rehearsal break from Ragtime.

Q. What type of dancing and dancers do you enjoy and look for?

A. I always hated the chorus lines. In my entire life I have always hated the chorus lines.. Maybe because I'm not from an American background. Maybe because I didn't grow up with the Rockettes. But anytime that I see people doing the same thing over and over again, I get so bored. It doesn't matter if it is wonderful. I get bored. And maybe the years and years of doing all the ballet and doing the same thing all over. So I look for individuals. I look for the acting ability into the jazz. I think that's partially, too, what Matt (Mattox) had and actually what Jack had. Jack Cole was the creator of it all. It gave personality. Jack had a great understanding of sexuality, for when you saw those women, those women dancing like men, but they were extremely feminine, but in a very earthy kind of way. Not pretty little girls. They were down there (the floor). And I loved that. And the same thing with the man. It

91

doesn't matter what the sexuality was personally, but when you saw them, they were like panthers. They were like warriors, and it was just so exciting to see that, to see both the feminine and the masculine onstage. I loved that, and those are the people that I keep on working, that I keep calling on.

He was a real genius. And you know, the saddest part is - sometimes I say Jack Cole and some kids say "Who?" That's really sad. They don't know, they really don't know. Even Bobby (Fosse) said many times to me, "Without Jack, where would I be? You know, I was in cabaret and strip business. Without Jack, where would I be..." The great ones know where they came from. Its different with Robbins. Robbins doesn't say it, but we know! (she laughs!)

Q. How is jazz dancing different today as compared to years ago?

A. Discipline! And that's the magic word in today's world. Maybe I'm getting old, but there was a discipline we took up. And I still do. I get up every morning and do my *barre*. I'm crinking and crying and screaming, but I still practice it because I feel better afterwards. As hard as it is for my body, it still feels like "Hey, now my blood is going, I can think better..."

It's something that we were taught to love. So it wasn't an imposition, it wasn't difficult at all. Not to me, not to people of my generation. I remember when we were doing the original *Chicago*, and Bobby (Fosse) used to come in at 1/2 hour, but then, I would go not at 1/2 hour, but at 1 hour before, like in the ballet world. I would take 1/2 hour to put my makeup on, and at 1/2 hour when everyone came in I would walk onstage and do a *barre*. And *Chicago* didn't have that much dancing, it was mostly Fosse, you know, sexy. But I did it, and I remember Bobby used to come, he used to sit on the steps and watch me and ask me questions about "Where did you get that?" because I had certain exercises from teachers from around the world. And he admired so much, the fact that I was there warming up. He said "You know, we don't do this!" I said "Some of us do, and some of us will continue doing it." Because it's not that you have to warm up your muscles, so you don't hurt yourself - not only that. It puts you in a frame of mind where you are focused and concentrated on your work, on your role, in your...you know, like a temple. And all I know is that I don't see it around me. I really don't see it.

Q. What are the wrong reasons to dance? What are the right reasons to dance?

A. Because I want to be famous, because I want to make a lot of money, because I want to win a Tony Award, because I want to be on Broadway. "Broadway is a street!" I say always, "nothing but the name of a street!" It doesn't necessarily have the best theatre in the world anyway. The best theatre in the world that happens on Broadway is usually taken from somewhere else. It's nothing but a street.

It's who you are, and it's because it gives me a freedom, because it exhilarates me, because it heightens my life - those are the reasons why we dance. Because it is an expression like nothing else. You don't need too many words when you know how to put in a gesture. The most magical moments on the stage, even in musicals where everybody sings, are those visual moments where something emotional is done with a gesture. And you have a perfect example in *West Side Story*. The most divine moment when they meet for the first time. It was nothing but a gesture - no words were uttered. Nobody was singing - he (Robbins) knew. The very end - what made you cry - was those two people going like this (a finger touch). It was a gesture - it wasn't even a step. It was a gesture. And that's what dance can do. Even if you don't do 32 fouettes, if you know what your body can do, and you express your emotions - then you go beyond the technique of your body. And you can express your emotions.

Somehow I'm glad I'm not from an American culture...one thing I hate on Broadway is when they (auditioners) go "Love me, love me, love me!" (She holds out her hands with a gesture that infers a need for attention). The moment they start doing that I hate them. Don't tell me that. Allow me to get into your world. If you are acting the piece, then I want to reach in, like *West Side Story*.

Q. Any finals thoughts on topics we have talked about?

A. My neighbor in the country, the kid in the country who mows the grass, cause he's good looking, he wants to come to L.A. to be an actor. He's never had an acting lesson. But you know, he's right. He could make it in television. That's the sad part. That's what I'm saying about supply and demand. You know, you did not get a job thirty years ago if you did not have a great technique. It didn't matter how good you looked. So we had to work very hard. We had to do it. I had to learn how to do knee slides, I had never done that, but you had to do it, because that's what was expected of dancers. Now, it isn't...the dancing demands are not the same. So, where do they go to work - to California, because they can do MTV and get a lot of money. That's what I'm saying, it's not the kids fault, it's nobody's fault, it's just that times have changed.

20
DONALD MCKAYLE –
JAZZ DANCE THEN AND NOW

Reprinted from *Dancer* with permission, Copyright June 1998

The origin of theatrical jazz dance is not that long ago. Many of the pioneers are still with us, making it imperative for their first hand experiences and recollections of the evolution of theatrical jazz dance to be recorded. One such person is dancer/choreographer Donald McKayle. Known for his classic modern dance works like *Rainbow*

Round My Shoulder and *Games*, he also worked with many of the pioneers of theatrical jazz dance as it was being formulated. His piece *District Storyville* made use of vernacular jazz movements in retelling the beginnings of jazz music in New Orleans. I was able to interview McKayle when he was in residence
with the Youth Performing Arts School in Louisville, KY, and this is his story of the beginnings of theatrical jazz dance.

"I started in the middle 1940s to take classes, and there was no jazz dancing as such being taught. There were people teaching tap - in Harlem especially - Norma Miller, Mary Bruce - and she had kids who could tap and do wonderful things. They were these lines of girls, basically, and there were groups of tap dancers. So those were the first kinds of lessons that would presage what we have today." McKayle noted that in the 1940s, there were classes in ballet, tap, acrobatics, modern, and ethnic dance, but no jazz classes to speak of. His early training came at the New Dance Group studio, at that time located on 59th between Madison and 5th Ave in New York City. There were classes in modern dance with Jean Erdman and Sophie Maslow, and within a one block radius were classes in Indian dance, flamenco, and the School of American Ballet. "Balanchine was starting, all of his work which led into Ballet Society and finally the New York City Ballet."

McKayle's first exposure to theatrical jazz dance was in niteclubs and in a concert organized by *NY Times* dance critic John Martin. Jack Cole was performing in niteclubs with Evelyn and Beatrice Kraft, presenting authentic East Indian dances that eventually he merged with the swing beat of the Lindy. He remembers the Martin concert as a benefit for the Spanish Refugee Appeal in the late 1940s at the Ziegfeld Theatre. "And it had Ethel and George Martin, Bob Alexander, Carol Haney - and they did *Sing, Sing, Sing*. It was fabulous (he laughs). 'Whoa, what is this!?'" he exclaimed at this new form of jazz inspired movements.

The lindy was very important to the Cole style and feel, according to McKayle. "Jack had lots of sequences based on the lindy, cause every time you auditioned for him, you had to do a lot of footwork. Which was based on the music and the shifting and partnering, but taken solely without a partner. I think he used that and just took it somewhere else." Along with most who rubbed shoulders with Cole, McKayle remembers him with fear as well as reverence. "Jack would put you through it, and you had to look like you could survive. And if you didn't survive, he would just run right over you. He was a scary guy!"

Like Cole, another modern dancer who ventured into early theatrical jazz was choreographer Daniel Nagrin. He was assistant to choreographer Helen Tamiris, later married to her, and he added a theatricality to modern dance, set to a contemporary theme, that McKayle saw as another early strain in theatrical jazz dance. "When I first worked with him (Nagrin), it was the end of the 1940s into the 1950s. He was assisting Helen and doing his own personal choreography. And so he developed things like *Strange Hero*, with the

Stan Kenton music, and it was all about the gangster as a hero in Hollywood. And it was a wonderfully theatrical dance, absolutely. And because he had this wonderful theatrical quality, he did not have a technique that was purely modern dance." It was another early use of jazz dance in a concert setting.

In the 1950s, choreographer Katherine Dunham had a school in New York City, but as Dunham was often on the road, classes were taken over by teacher Syvilla Fort. "She dealt with the blues, swing, things like that, and there were, of course, dances of the Caribbean." But McKayle feels that the Dunham school training was not ideally suited for the dance demands of Broadway. "A lot of people who were on Broadway went to her classes, but there was no 'step' if you trained with Dunham that you would do on Broadway."

Interestingly, McKayle credits a non-jazz dancer with early creation of a need for theatrical jazz dance. "Maybe the person most responsible for that who had nothing to do with jazz dance was Agnes de Mille. Because she was the first choreographer that made dance an absolutely unique element in a show." He feels that by making dance a creative element rather than just a diversion, there became an instant demand for concert choreographers on Broadway. Modern dancers like Tamiris and Hanya Holm, ballet choreographers like Michael Kidd and Jerome Robbins, and the jazz dancers Cole and Fosse. Now dancers had to be trained in technique and expression as well as just displaying marginal ability and good looks. Acting skills were important, also, in the need to create characters who danced.

West Side Story (1957) is often cited as a pivotal point in theatrical jazz dance history, due to the ingenious use of jazz, ballet, and social dance by Jerome Robbins. But McKayle, who worked as dance captain and swing dancer with the original cast, sees the contribution of jazz movements differently than most historians. "I was in *West Side Story*, the original, and that wasn't jazz dance. It was very theatrical, quite marvelous, but the part that was closest to jazz is what Peter Gennaro (assistant choreographer) did. Of course, Jerome Robbins took all of the bows for Peter's work. It was Peter's work that was closest to jazz dance. 'America' was Peter's, all of the Shark movement in the gymnasium was Peter's...he was an unsung hero. I think he was terrific. What a fine choreographer."

Another of McKayle's favorites is choreographer Talley Beatty. In 1959, Beatty choreographed *The Road of the Phoebe Snow*. Set to music by Duke Ellington and Billy Strayhorn, the 30 minute piece was about life on the wrong side of the tracks. Also by Beatty is 1960's *Come and Get the Beauty of It Hot*, set to Dizzy Gillespie, Charles Mingus, and Gil Evans, and in the 1970s he staged many Broadway shows. McKayle said "All of Talley Beatty's pieces were set to jazz music and were fierce, you know. I think he was a very good choreographer in terms of theatrical jazz. One of the best. And way ahead of a lot of other people. He's gone now, but his work lasts."

As for today's theatrical jazz dance, McKayle is both optimistic and worried. "I think that at this point to see jazz so strong in the universities means that it has established itself. There's still certain places you can hit a problem because of people who are just backward, and think that jazz is not worthy. So, I always speak up...there is prejudice, in terms of the newspapers and everything. We have to get past all of that. And it takes time. I think time is compressed now, so I don't think it will take us long. " But it is refreshing to McKayle to see new individual movements in jazz dance, similar to those of the 1940s and 1950s. Of Savion Glover in *Bring In 'da Noise, Bring In 'da Funk*, he says "he makes a point of saying that tap dancing that has lines and class was kind of diluting what he calls 'da beat.' It will take awhile for all of that to find its own center. And it's all healthy. I like to see this kind of discussion."

Which is fine for more vernacular styles, but for theatrical jazz dance, McKayle is quick to emphasize the need for formal technique. "It's different from vernacular dance, where you have to have a wonderful strong rhythm structure, like people like Savion Glover. They're not interested in whether you straighten your knee or point your foot. That's not what it's about. It's about beat and interaction. But when you go into theatrical jazz, you have to have all those other things. You have to have a sense of line and formation. The kind of things you expect in the theatre."

As someone who has made a life in dance and theatre, and experienced a range of styles and philosophies, Donald McKayle treats it all with devotion and respect. Dancing is not a passing fad, but an essential force that lives within. "To me, passion is so essential...it hurts any kind of dance when there's no artistry. There are just feats." After living through the then and now of jazz dance, he sees the future of jazz dance as depending on absorbing the new, and preserving the old. "I am always glad when I see new movement, it's just I hate this sort of throwing out the old as if it was garbage, you know? You have to preserve and build, rather than remove and replace. As in any technique."

21
LAST CHAPTER – FINAL *DANCER* COLUMN

Reprinted from *Dancer* with permission, Copyright July 1998

For the last 2 1/2 years, I have been privileged to have my thoughts on jazz dance published in *Dancer* newspaper. Thanks to the generosity of editor Owen Goldman, my comments, sometimes inflammatory but always sincere, have appeared on a regular basis, celebrating the accomplishments of jazz dancers and urging others to think and act seriously about this much loved and much maligned art form.

However, this will be my last column. My work as a professor at Western Kentucky University and other new ideas are clamoring for my time. One project is a course on the History of Jazz Dance, taught entirely via the Internet. Set for Spring semester of 1999, this course will examine the evolution of jazz dance from African origins to the Broadway and concert stage. Jazz dancers, for the first time, will now have the opportunity to study their heritage in a university level course, from any location in the world. All that is needed is a computer, modem, and Internet access.

A book on the golden age of theatrical jazz dance, 1940-1960, is also planned. But the biggest project in mind is the formation of the Jazzart Jazz Dance Company. Based in New York and here in Bowling Green, KY, this company will tour with artistic jazz dance pieces and arts in education programs.

When I began writing this column, my idea was to present jazz dance as a dance form worthy of serious study and debate. So little has been written in the past, and today most periodicals give little exposure to jazz dance. But there is so much to write about, and so many people doing commendable work. In two years, the stellar list of those interviewed included Donald McKayle, Graciela Daniele, Marcus Alford

101

and Annie Day, Billy Siegenfeld, Jeannie Hill, Chet Walker, Benny Bell, Danny Buraczeski, Michele Moss, Maurice Curry, and Vicki Willis. Dance companies included Spectrum Dance Theater, Decided Jazz Danceworks, Jump Rhythm Jazz Project, Jazz Dance America, and JAZZDANCE. Broadway shows and new forms included *The Fosse Project, Stomp, Bring In 'da Noise Bring in 'da Funk, Jam on the Groove, Jazz Dance LA*, and the World Jazz Dance Congress. And of course, there is the article on *Teachers on the Frontline*, highlighting the efforts of every jazz dance teacher inspiring youngsters and adults in local studios.

This list is not an effort to boast, but rather to show the richness and appeal of jazz dance in America. Jazz dance is a major component of artistic and commercial dance worldwide, and deserves to be noted, studied, and understood. There are hundreds of remarkable people in jazz dance who have a story to tell, and they should be written down for others to learn from and be inspired by. I could write a monthly column every day and still not come close to making a dent in documenting the effect of jazz dance on the American culture and people.

If there is any common theme to be gleaned from the comments of this remarkable group of jazz dancers, I would say it was the passion with which they work, and the respect they have for the art form. For instance, Benny Bell, teacher and choreographer of Afro-Jazz said "In our profession we are like slaves - 'oh my god, we've got to keep the numbers up or they will go to aerobics!' They have made us virtually doormats. And I say if I have to be a doormat, I will be nothing at all. And I say 'here's your money - get out.' Because this is what I do."

Michele Moss of Decidedly Jazz Danceworks concurring that "the spirit of jazz - that is something very important to us. Not archival, but something that honors the history and ancestry, and keeps us moving to the future, and is innovative." And Chet Walker of *The Fosse Project*, talking of work attitudes: "In the present generation, you want to get it - get it and move on. I came from a generation where that's not true. You were constantly striving to get it. You held the idea that the dancer could always do better and worked constantly to improve. Mr. Fosse would say in *Dancin'*, for example, if you ever thought you did a perfect show, you should really hand in your notice. It's impossible, and that's kind of cool, to keep working to perfection."

Then there is Graciela Daniele, choreographer of Broadway's *Ragtime*, on the wrong reasons to dance - "Because I want to be famous, because I want to make a lot of money, because I want to win a Tony award, because I want to be on Broadway. 'Broadway is a street!' I always say, 'nothing but the name of a street!'. And on the right reasons to dance - "It's WHO you are, and because it gives me a freedom, because it exhilarates me, because it heightens my life - those are the reasons why we dance. Because it is an expression like nothing else."

I feel that her thoughts on the right reasons cuts to the heart of the appeal of jazz dance. Simply put, jazz dance is an expression like no other. Jazz dance starts with feeling from the heart and soul of our existence. It can take us from the ecstasy of release to the lowest of the blues, from spine shaking syncopation to the slinky seduction of a muted jazz mood. Jazz dance takes what is inside of us, and puts it on display for all to see. We relive common thoughts and communicate feelings we all share. It exhilarates, it heightens. It's free.

Some would like to put a damper on jazz dance for this very reason. Often art is considered as something that we should think about, rather than feel. Art resides in the brain, not the soul. But if art is anything, it is a communication of a common thing, whether it be a thought, feeling, or emotion. Jazz dance has the feeling and the emotion.

What we need to do now is encourage those who communicate the jazz feeling. It could be in a dance concert, or a Broadway show, or a local dance recital. Treating jazz dance with respect is where the future lies, and in using jazz dance as a basis of communication between people. Jazz dance is likeable, and can be entertaining. But, like Benny Bell, we must adopt that attitude that you do jazz dance the right way, or don't do it at all. Like Michele Moss, we must examine the history of jazz dance and use it as a springboard to speak of the future. Like Chet Walker and Bob Fosse, we should not settle for just "getting it" - let's work to perfection. And like Graciela Daniele, we must not dance for the wrong reasons - let's dance for freedom, exhilaration, and an expression like no other. Like these great jazz dance artists, we too must work with passion and respect.

To close out this column and my tenure as a writer for *Dancer*, I would like to leave you with one more philosophical thought. First, because it is my opinion that jazz dance is lacking in philosophy, and second, because there is one more quote, not from an interview but from *Jazz Danceology* by Marcus Alford, that states the case on jazz dance. Matt Mattox, one of the pioneers of jazz dance performance and education, says:

There is a joy and a pleasure in jazz dance, even as there is in jazz music, that you will not find in any other form of dance. There is a freedom, a liberation, that cannot be found in another style. In this freedom and liberation is a form of creativity. This creativity is a personal expression of individuality. This individuality is without limitation. This discipline, liberation, and freedom without limitation is 'jazz dance'...a true art form.

22
ALL THAT'S JAZZ

by Bob Boross

Reprinted with permission of *Dance Magazine*, Copyright 1999

Jazz dance can express the pulse of society while expressing the longings of an individual. It has undergone myriad changes throughout its short existence, evolving a variety of techniques to express many moods in a wide range of styles. Here are a few of the innovators who have developed jazz dance.

"Jazz is a feeling," proclaims Nat Horne, veteran of sixteen Broadway shows. "Jazz" says teacher Matt Mattox, "is a skillful combination of both rhythm and design." Jazz dance, according to choreographer Danny Buraczeski, is a melting pot of countless styles and influences.

Like a child of mixed heritage, today's jazz dance retains aspects of its multiple roots. But despite its dual parentage in African and European traditions, jazz dance is strictly an American creation--a twentieth-century invention that personifies the social, technological, and visual history of popular American culture.

Jazz dance and music originated jointly, at the beginning of the century, in a lower-class neighborhood in New Orleans called District Storyville. The American public was charmed by the heightened rhythmic qualities and by the 1920s, aided by mass migration of Southern blacks to Northern cities and mass media inventions such as the radio and phonograph, jazz reigned supreme in America and Europe. The rhythmic punch of jazz music and dance provided the perfect accompaniment to the accelerating pace of the Roaring Twenties.

At that time jazz dance was performed by individuals at dance halls, at rent parties during the Depression, and on Broadway and vaudeville stages by dance "acts," who recreated social jazz dancing into formalized routines. Many reviewers criticized jazz for not having artistic dance value, while others, such as early jazz dance writer Mura Dehn, saw it as both high art and folk art. She believed the golden age of jazz dance was from the 1920s to the 1940s. Dehn proposed that the movement of jazz dance was improvisational and was an individual's reaction to the rhythmic feeling inherent in the interplay of jazz music's steady and syncopated beats.

In the 1940s, when American society was transformed by World War II, jazz music evolved into a more complicated form known as bebop. On Broadway, jazz dance that was derived from social styles vanished with the emerging popularity of ballet and modern dance. Dance no longer was seen as spectacle, but rather as a vehicle for advancing the plot.

From 1936 through the 1960s, choreographers from the ballet and modern dance worlds - George Balanchine, Agnes de Mille, Jack Cole, Hanya Holm, Helen Tamiris, Michael Kidd, Jerome Robbins, and Bob Fosse--created a very demanding offshoot of jazz dance that surpassed the technical skills of the chorine or dance act and required instead a trained dancer. In this form (loosely termed modern jazz, theatrical jazz, and sometimes "freestyle"), the dancer was more imitative than individual. The ability to execute movements set by the choreographer was more important than the dancer's skill at improvisation.

At the same time, concert choreographers Alvin Ailey, Katherine Dunham, and Daniel Nagrin were setting pieces inspired by jazz but still dependent on ballet and modern dance techniques. Since the application of jazz dance had veered from improvisation to imitation, there was a demand for a dancer who could quickly digest this hybrid of jazz and concert. A variety of techniques designed to train the new dancer materialized to meet this demand. Modern jazz dance was "in," hitting every studio like wildfire in the middle 1950s. Like a fledgling chick whose wings had not fully sprouted, the modern-jazz class was a hodgepodge of influences--ballet, jazz, jazzy jazz, or just about any style of ethnic dance done to jazz music.

TEACHERS AND CHOREOGRAPHERS

Teacher and choreographer Ruth Walton, who identified more with the concert stage than with Broadway, was a modern jazz dance innovator. She taught a technique class in the early 1950s that consisted of floor movements, a *barre* of stretching and limbering exercises, center floor exercises, across-the-floor locomotor movements, and jazz footwork. Her class culminated with two short dance phrases composed by the teacher and two student improvisations.

Jack Cole was a film and Broadway choreographer working in this new jazz form. After being trained at Denishawn in the 1930s, Cole struck out on his own, adding classes in East Indian and other ethnic dance forms while jiving with Lindy dancers at Harlem's Savoy Ballroom. From 1944 to 1948, as a choreographer at Columbia Pictures in Hollywood, Cole was permitted to train a group of dancers under contract for studio film assignments. Some of those dancers in his daily classes were Gwen Verdon, Carol Haney, George and Ethel Martin, and Bob Alexander. It was, in effect, a Jack Cole dance company, with technical training that included classes in Cecchetti ballet, Humphrey-Weidman modern dance, gymnastics, East Indian, Cuban, and flamenco ethnic forms. Although there has never been a codification of this technique, his extraordinary standard became synonymous with the highest level of modern jazz dance training.

In 1954 Bob Fosse burst onto the Broadway scene with his show-stopping "Steam Heat" in *The Pajama Game*. It generated a demand for classes in a Broadway style of modern jazz dance. Peter Gennaro, a dancer in "Steam Heat," gave classes that began with a ballet *barre* and progressed to across-the-floor combinations and a jazzy center combination that emphasized his unique fast footwork.

Teacher Frank Wagner added precision and isolation to his jazz classes. Jon Gregory taught without a set format, preferring free-form

107

general warm-up exercises that led to a wild jazzy combination. Although popular, these classes also did not result in a codified jazz technique and therefore are no longer practiced.

New York City was not the sole mecca for jazz dancing. Hollywood provided work for many dancers in the film industry. Eugene Facciuto, now known the world over as "Luigi," was a youthful tap dancer, acrobat, and singer who moved to Hollywood in the mid-1940s. There, he studied with renowned ballet teachers--Adolph Bolm, Bronislava Nijinska, Eugene Loring, and Edward Caton - but in 1946 he suffered a near-fatal car accident that resulted in paralysis. His rehabilitation consisted of ballet exercises executed with particular attention to body placement and positioning. Classes with "Miss Edith Jane" returned him to health and a career in films performing with Gene Kelly and Donald O'Connor. Dancers on the movie lot would do his class as a warm-up. By 1951 Luigi was giving classes in his movement technique in Hollywood. Then, in 1956, he came to New York City as an assistant on a Broadway show and began teaching his modern jazz dance technique at the June Taylor Dance Studio. Many dancers have adopted his technique, and his work has been codified and taught worldwide.

Also in the 1950s, Eugene Loring's American School of Dance in Los Angeles provided an opportunity for Cole and Matt Mattox to teach jazz. Loring himself gave classes in "freestyle"--a combination of ballet and modern, taught with a jazz-based vocabulary to jazz music. But of the three--Loring, Cole, and Mattox--it was Mattox who established a technique that has had global impact. After a stellar career as a dancer in films, he came to New York City in 1955 to work on Broadway, choreograph, and teach. He devised a series of exercises to train a dancer in body isolations with a jazz feeling, while still maintaining the format of a ballet class and a relationship between the *barre* and center floor combinations. Mattox's technique, in the Cole tradition, is demanding mentally as well as physically. He settled in France in 1975 and has codified his work, producing teachers who train jazz dancers in his technique throughout Europe and America.

In Chicago, Gus Giordano, who based his technique on modern

dance, has become a mainstay on the educational scene since the 1970s. Influenced in his childhood by the music of Jelly Roll Morton, Giordano moved to New York to work on Broadway and study with Holm, Alwin Nikolais, and Dunham. In 1953, he relocated to Evanston, Illinois, and began a school. Giordano developed a class that started with strong floorwork in the Holm tradition, emphasizing the qualities of strength from the floor and including an undulating movement that emanated from the pelvis and rolled through the chest and arms. Codified in the mid-1970s, his technique now stands at the forefront of training in studios and universities throughout the world. In 1990 he established the yearly Jazz Dance World Congress, which includes training sessions and festival performances by internationally renowned jazz dance companies.

CONTEMPORARY JAZZ DANCE

The 1950s witnessed the birth and explosion of theatrical jazz dance, but the evolution of Broadway, film, and television and the emergence of MTV and videos have changed its execution and personality. Although Luigi, Mattox, and Giordano continue to teach, many teachers and choreographers have either used these masters' inventions as a starting point and adapted their techniques or have created training methods that reflect visions of their own. A short list would include Charles Kelley, Frank Pietri, Joe Tremaine, Roland Dupree, Camilla Long Hill, Lou Conte, Frank Hatchett, Phil Black, Lea Darwin, Rhett Dennis, Liz Williamson, and Lynn Simonson.

Modern dance and ballet have supported contemporary choreographers with an interest in jazz dance and music, among them Danny Buraczeski, Margo Sappington, Twyla Tharp, Garth Fagan, and Peter Pucci. The Toronto choreographer Danny Grossman has drawn from his teenage interest in the "beatnik" jazz of the late 1950s and a decade of work with Paul Taylor to create modern dances accompanied by jazz music. He has set his piece *Higher* to a suite of bluesy Ray Charles songs and *Magneto-Dynamo* to a pulsating, hard-driving score by bassist Charles Mingus.

Although jazz dance's evolution in the last fifty years has traveled from social and traditional forms to collaborations with the concert techniques of ballet and modern, a recent trend has seen the renewal of jazz's authentic rhythmic feeling. A recent pioneer is Billy Siegenfeld, a professor at Northwestern University, who advocates a return to the philosophy of traditional jazz dance where rhythm is the motivating factor for movement. His Jump Rhythm Jazz Technique focuses on making the body a total rhythm instrument by instilling in his dancers a razor-sharp rhythmic sensibility. This allows for the exploration of various parts of the body as instruments in displaying the accents and "hits" of jazz music. Siegenfeld seeks to lay bare the emotional content of the rhythm; therefore, technical virtuosity as in standard movement vocabularies is not the goal. Instead, his movement, a genuine reaction to syncopated jazz rhythms, signals a return to the heritage of classic jazz dancing.

Because of the complexity of rhythms and isolations, many jazz teachers advocate that the serious study of jazz dance begin in a student's teen years, when the dancer is better able to grasp its intricate nature. A few years of prior training in ballet or modern can be beneficial to the progress of the student. Jazz dance radiates a musicality, a physicality, and at times a sensuality that requires some maturity.

But in order to understand and master jazz dance, a student must be open to the variety of its expression. Because jazz is many things to many people, it cannot possess a single technique. As in modern dance, jazz takes shape in techniques that have withstood the test of time. From its folk origins and the innovations of the masters to the work of today's classic and contemporary artists, jazz dance lives in the techniques, styles, and personalities of many practitioners. Individuals have used the form to train dancers for the concert and commercial stage, as well as to provide an outlet for recreational dancers who want to express their joys and pain, hopes and sorrows, and all of the feelings within their souls.

23
IMPROVING ARTISTRY IN
JAZZ DANCE CHOREOGRAPHY

by Bob Boross

Reprinted from *Dance Teacher* magazine with permission, Copyright March 2001

A ballet choreographer creates a "ballet." A modern dance choreographer creates a "piece." But a choreographer working in the field of jazz dance has often labels his work a "number," a term dating back to a time when jazz and show dances were offered as frivolous entertainment on vaudeville and revue stages. Jazz dances were meant to be energetic, snappy, and fun - primarily displaying humor and pizzazz. But jazz as a serious work of art? Well, rarely, if ever. Jazz dance was known for its bubbly appeal but not for artistic qualities or inventive staging.

Still, in a development similar to that of ballet where movements from folk dancing were adapted for the stage, many choreographers from the world of artistic dance have perceived a value in the movement vocabulary of jazz dance as source material for more artistic works. As far back as the 1930s, jazz historian Mura Dehn gave concerts in New York City demonstrating how jazz dancing was really a folk dance, expressing the culture and feelings of its originators. Choreographers from modern dance quickly saw the value of jazz dance in creating an atmosphere and characters based on urban personalities. One such was Daniel Nagrin in his piece *Strange Hero*, which portrayed an urban street tough guy, and another was Katherine Dunham in her work *Le Jazz Hot*. Ballet choreographers adapting jazz movements for the musical theatre stage included George Balanchine in *On Your Toes* and Jerome Robbins in *On The Town*. Of course, the original jazz dance pioneer Jack Cole combined a background in modern and ethnic dance with the movements of lindy hoppers to create the Broadway jazz dance idiom. Other choreographers who used jazz dance for artistic dance were Alvin Ailey, Talley Beatty, and Donald McKayle.

So it is possible to say that jazz dance has a lighthearted appeal, but is also capable of expressing feelings in an artistic sense. What it does not inherently have, and what was provided by many of the artistic dancemakers listed above, is a method of choreographic structure and creation of movement. It is a lack of knowledge on the part of jazz dance choreographers in this key area that has slowed the progress of jazz dance as an art form (although jazz choreographers can hardly be faulted as the demands placed on early show choreographers did not require possessing such a knowledge). Jazz choreographers may know jazz, but they may not be skilled in the various approaches to artistic choreography. Therefore it is beneficial to jazz choreographers who want to create more sophisticated work to first study the basic laws of dance composition, and to examine how elements that are singular to jazz dance can be utilized to create a dance piece that is both artistic and jazz.

There are two easily accessible ways to unlock the mysteries of choreography, and I make use of both when I teach classes in Choreography for Jazz Dance at the University of California, Irvine. One is to study the writings of one of the first choreographers to codify a method for dance composition – the modern dance trailblazer Doris Humphrey. In her book *The Art of Making Dances*, Humphrey outlines the various components of dancemaking at a level that is suitable for the beginner to understand. Every aspiring jazz dance choreographer would gain a considerable understanding of the components of dance composition by reading her classic book.

To briefly summarize her approach, Humphrey separates dance into four components – design, dynamics, rhythm, and motivation. All effective dance composition, she feels, contains elements of these categories, and it is the job of the choreographer to recognize how each component can be manipulated to enhance the choreographer's desired effect. Another pearl of wisdom she offers concerns phrasing, or creating movement passages that explain one succinct thought in a time span that is easily digested by the spectator. Phrases are like sentences. Each phrase should contain one thought, logically grow out of the previous phrase, and flow seamlessly into the next.

The other way to unlock the mystery of choreography is simply to watch good choreography – over and over again. Once you know the basics as outlined by Humphrey, the aspiring choreographer should watch choreography of all genres, not just jazz, to see how phrasing and Humphrey's four components are manipulated in making dance pieces. A natural inquisitiveness is part of the learning process, and much can be gleaned from observing masters like George Balanchine, Martha Graham, Paul Taylor, Jerome Robbins, and Bob Fosse. An excellent example of an artistic jazz dance is the piece *Lonely Street, Lonely Town* by Robert North. This piece appears on the videotape *An Evening with the Ballet Rambert*.

Assuming that the budding jazz choreographer has acquired the skills of dance composition as outlined by Humphrey, it is now time to turn thoughts to aspects of choreography that are specific to jazz movement. Or, what are the elements of dance composition that apply more to jazz dance than to other forms?

In terms of design, the choreographer should be choosing movements and positions that are inspired by the heritage of jazz dance vocabulary. S/he may opt for a literal characterization of time eras by choosing well known steps like the Charleston ('20s), Lindy ('30s), Frug ('60s), or Breakdancing ('80s). Or s/he may choose another method of creating movement that is central to jazz dance – that is, how does the rhythm of the music make you feel. Although ballet is presupposed with form and modern dance with a more mental approach to creating a piece, jazz dancers react to their music by moving in a way that expresses how the rhythm is *felt*. This approach involves a heightened use of dynamics and rhythm. It may inspire movements that merely amplify the accents of the music. Or the dancer may create a unique rhythm that is placed over the beat of the music much like a jazz musician does during an improvisation. In either fashion, the choreographer is using improvisation to create a movement that is directly related to the rhythm of the music being danced to. If the movement reaction is true, the result will be movement that honestly reflects the dancer's feelings. This feeling based approach to movement is the prime way that composition for jazz dance differs from that of modern dance and ballet.

Another method of choosing movements refers back to Humphrey's fourth aspect of composition - motivation. The accomplished choreographer will most likely have a mental outline of the proposed piece that examines its overall purpose and the transitions in emotions that occur during the process of exploring the theme. The choreographer determines "What is the dance character trying to say at that very moment? How does that expression fit into the overall theme of the piece?" Once done, the choreographer should then be choosing movements that depict the exact emotion or feeling. By following the axiom of always choosing movement that has a direct motivation, the choreographer can be assured that each movement will have a real meaning and therefore have an impact on the audience.

Common mistakes of beginning choreographers are usually related to a lack of ability in manipulating the components of design, dynamics, rhythm, motivation, and of phrasing. The choreographer may be choosing movements or arrangements of dancers that are too similar and therefore do not provide enough variety in order to continually engage the imagination of the audience (poor design). Or the dance may be a nonstop barrage of hard accents or rapid fire, choppy movements (no variation in dynamics or rhythm). A section of choreography may seem to go one forever without a break or change in movement so that the viewer cannot see how the initial movements are related to the final movements (improper use of phrasing).

A problem that is seen over and over in the work of jazz choreographers is related to movement that does not have a clear motivation. Rather than thinking in terms of motivation while choreographing, often the jazz dancer will revert to choosing standard movements from technique classes, like *pas de bourees* or *battements*, or even trick movements. The worst example of this is when a switch split or, the most recent offense, the *fouetté* turn, is inserted into a dance for no logical reason. Yes, these movements will display the ability of the dancer, but if there is no logical reason for the trick to be inserted into the dance, then leave it out. If the movement choice does not emerge from the theme and the motivation of the dance, then it should not be considered as a viable choice. Your piece will be better without it.

Seeing jazz dance in an artistic light can be offsetting at first, and will be a challenge to the choreographer. It takes fortitude and concentration to delve deeply into the motivations for movements. But choreographers are often surprised at how easily the transition can be made from stock jazz choreography to artistic jazz choreography. And they are also surprised at how fulfilling the results are, both to the choreographer and to the audience. What it takes to accomplish the switch is an increased knowledge and understanding of the tools of dance composition, and the desire to step back from the traditional approach to jazz dancing and grow into a new, more satisfying one. Saying more with your choreography is always the goal of the choreographer. By following the paths blazed by Doris Humphrey and many other proficient choreographers, this goal is within that grasp of all jazz dance choreographers.

24
ESSENTIALS OF THE FREESTYLE JAZZ DANCE OF MATT MATTOX

by Bob Boross

Reprinted from *Dance Teacher* magazine with permission, Copyright July 2002

In today's world of hip hop dance, the term "freestyle" is used to describe the act when a dancer creates movement through improvisation. But as far back as the 1940s, the noted film and ballet choreographer Eugene Loring taught classes in what he defined as "freestyle dance." Freestyle was used to describe a form of movement that was primarily jazz dance, but that borrowed heavily from ballet, modern, tap, and ethnic dance movement. The new name was meant to distinguish the form from authentic jazz dancing,

Although not its founder, there is one person who has carried the torch for freestyle dance more than any other. He is the dancer who was a protégé of both Jack Cole and Loring, and one who has led the field of jazz dance on an international level for more than 45 years – the teacher, performer, and choreographer Matt Mattox.

Matt Mattox has been called a legend in the field of jazz dance, one of the pioneers in bringing jazz to the Broadway and concert stage. Depending on their age, most dancers have experienced or witnessed the talents of Mattox in one form or another. In the 1940s and 1950s, he was a featured dancer in film musicals, partnering Cyd Charisse, Marilyn Monroe, Gwen Verdon, Lucille Ball, and June Allyson. His most notable role was as Caleb in *Seven Brides for Seven Brothers*, the feisty third brother whose split jumps electrified the film's wild barn raising dance. In the 1960s, Mattox choreographed Broadway and television shows, and emerged as one of the top teachers of theatrical jazz dance in America.

Thousands of dancers flocked to his studio in New York City, and both the Dance Educators of America and the Dance Masters of America showered awards on Mattox for creating a codified training technique for jazz dancing.

In the 1970s and 1980s, Mattox moved to Europe, spreading his teaching technique and founding the concert jazz dance group *JazzArt*. He is credited with catalyzing the jazz dance boom in Europe during this time. Since then, Mattox has remained active as a teacher and choreographer on both continents. He has recently returned to America as an invited teacher at the Jazz Dance World Congress, The Jazzart Jazz Dance Technique and Choreography Festival, the American Dance Festival, and in the summer of 2001 at The Jacob's Pillow Dance Festival and the Boston Summer  Dance Festival. His freestyle jazz dance technique, a highly intricate and challenging method for training dancers for the professional theatre and dance companies, has been at the center of his appearances at these renowned dance festivals.

Although he is known throughout the world as a master of jazz dance, Mattox feels that it is more accurate to call his work "freestyle" rather than jazz. As a choreographer he wants to be free to draw from any movement form experienced during his eclectic career. Not just relegated to authentic or traditional jazz dancing, his movement shows influences from all forms of dance. He prefers to let the music to which he is choreographing create a feeling or sensation within his body, and this feeling will determine in what form his movement will take shape. The movement of Mattox often has a basis in what has historically been called jazz dance, but it still transcends authentic jazz dance.

Mattox points to his varied technical training as the justification for his freestyle jazz approach. He began his studies as a tap dancer in his teen years, and then moved on to become a ballet dancer of such proficiency that in the 1950s he was repeatedly asked by Ballet Theatre director Lucia Chase to join the company as a soloist. But Mattox credits his years as a dancer with Jack Cole as his most influential. Professional work with Cole completed his training in jazz dance, modern, and in ethnic dance forms. By the time he decided to begin choreographing and teaching on his own, Mattox was thoroughly accomplished in all forms of theatrical dance.

The life work of Mattox as a freestyle jazz dance artist covers vast areas – his approaches to choreography and his movement style, and the method by which he trains his dancers to move in his fashion – his "technique." But it is possible to indentify some key concepts that describe the overall look and execution of the way that Mattox moves. They are - moving in *plié*, isolating body parts, using a unique approach to weight transfer, heightening the use of dynamics and rhythm, dancing in a relaxed state, and executing movement with the utmost in energy, passion, and feeling. Now, how does Mattox create his dancers? Just what is involved in his freestyle jazz dance technique? Here are some of the fundamental elements that Mattox has voiced as cornerstones of his technique class.

LENGTHENING BODY LINES

At first look his class seems to contain standard elements of many jazz dance classes - *pliés, tendús, developpés*, and leg extensions. His students stretch on the floor, practice jumps and turns, and work on a combination at the end of the class. But there are special ways of executing those exercises that develop the remarkable aspects of Mattox's movement style. The first is that all lines of the body lengthen during exercises. Mattox encourages the dancer to envision being inside of a sphere that just touches the fingers and toes when the arms and legs are outstretched. The dancer is to lengthen the lines of the arms, legs, and neck by stretching from the shoulders, hip sockets, and spine - pushing the fingers, toes, and head through the sphere, in order to disturb new space as the body is made longer. The movement is downward into the floor as well as upward and outward. The dancer becomes taller from supporting more in the hamstring and gluteus of the standing leg. The arm becomes longer not through a stiffened stretch of the fingers, but by increasing the stretch from the shoulder joint. The same method applies to making the leg longer, by stretching from the hip socket on down to the toes. The end result is a dancer who is enlivened by the multi-directional lines of energy, all exuding from the pelvis and center through the appendages and out through the sphere. The dancer is more impressive to the audience due to the longer lines and more energetic approach.

COMPLEXITY IN PATTERNS OF MOVEMENT

Another aspect is that of the rapidly changing directions of the lines of the movement. *Tendús* alternate with coordinating arm movements in eight positions on a count by count basis. From this the dancer gains knowledge of placement of arms and legs that create clean lines in space and the ability to move through these lines at will. It is an education in Mattox's sense of spatial design, one that rectifies his influences of curving and soft lines from classical ballet and sharp straight ones from jazz dance. The mind is challenged to learn multiple patterns of movement and to simultaneously execute the various rhythmic timings and patterns. By mastering these patterns of movement, the dancer learns independent control of all parts of the body.

ISOLATION

This leads to another chief aspect of Mattox's freestyle technique – isolation. The Mattox class teaches how to move individual parts of the body, whether in *tendús*, arm movements, or body parts like shoulders, hips, and rib cage. There are even isolation exercises for fingers, the cervical spine, and the foot's metatarsal joints. Jack Cole demanded in his dancers the ability to isolate individual body parts in order to execute his jazz style, as well as his East Indian dances. Mattox has created exercises that give his dancers that critical ability. A concentration in isolated body movement is present in all Mattox exercises.

WEIGHT TRANSFER IN PLIÉ

Within the class exercises, dancers move through various positions in all levels - *plié*, flat, and *relevé*. Balance must be maintained in all levels, and this is accomplished by the centering of weight through the hip sockets. No matter what position the dancer is in or is moving to, the hip sockets are to be in alignment with the supporting leg or legs. Most dancers understand this concept when on a flat level or in *relevé*, but many fail when they move into a low *plié* level. Often dancers will release the pelvis when entering *plié* and let the ribs push forward. They get lower by compromising the alignment of the upper body. Instead, the weight of the lower level should be felt at the bottom of the pelvis, balanced on the support of the thigh bones. The spine stays vertically lifted away from this weight. The pelvis feels lower to the ground, and the alignment of the spine is not compromised. When the dancer is aligned and centered in this fashion, he can move throughout the *plié* level with balance and smooth locomotion, and without distorted body positions.

HEIGHTENED DYNAMICS AND RHYTHM

Once a Mattox dancer masters the intricate patterns of the exercises, he is then instructed in the dynamic and rhythmic execution of those exercises. There are variations in attack and accent – sharp and slow, smooth and hard, movements over time and those performed in the blink of an eye. The dancer again is challenged by rhythmic patterns that change accents unpredictably, so that keeping up with the unusual beats forces the dancer to be lively and alert. They cannot be properly mastered by a dancer who is lethargic. A Mattox dancer is kinetically charged - his mind completely in the present moment, ready to absorb and execute any movement given by a choreographer.

RELAXATION AND REFLEX

A related concept is the movement quality of relaxation and reflex. Mattox once said that the ballerina Vera Zorina gave him a book with a photo of Nijinsky perched effortlessly in mid leap. On this photo she inscribed "Here, Matt, is the secret of all good dancing – relaxation!" Mattox has since imbued all of his work with the intention of executing his movement without unnecessary muscle tension. Movements should flow easily, without restriction. A way of achieving this is by approaching movement with reflex action. A reflex is a spontaneous, natural movement that happens without prior thought or preparation. Due to the instantaneous execution, the mind and muscles react in their most natural way, to direct the movement without extraneous actions. When a dancer is able to work in such a fashion, the movements become economical and more supple. A hallmark of Mattox's freestyle dance and technique is the appearance of a lack of effort being expended by the dancer, even while performing physically taxing movements. Relaxation and reflex action allow this to occur.

FREESTYLE MOVEMENT STYLE

It is difficult to separate the movement style of Mattox from his movement technique. There is a look to his choreography – an uncommon fusion of balanced and stimulating lines – that is also seen in his technique exercises. This is probably the most defining aspect of what "freestyle" jazz dance is. It's the look of the dancer in positions that have a jazz feel but also somewhat of a balletic impression. Not in the sense of recreating complete classical positions, but more indirectly - in the carriage of the torso and arms, and the centering of the weight while still in *plié*. The positions look jazzy and energetic due to isolations and off-center lines, but they also have a classic, timeless feeling due to the clean spatial lines of the torso, arms, and feet, and the lift in the spine. It is a way of movement that rectifies the sensual heritage of jazz dance with the classicism of the concert stage. The works of artists like Picasso and Stravinsky have been enhanced by the introduction of elements of jazz feeling. Mattox has done the same for classical dance, and created a ballet/jazz hybrid that he calls freestyle.

122

POWER, PASSION, AND EMOTION

The introduction to the freestyle mentality begins in the technique portion of the class, but it comes into full flower during the final combination. Mattox creates movement that utilizes all of the abilities developed in the class exercises. At this time, though, he most emphasizes dancing with full power, passion, and feeling. The dancer should be drawing from deep inner emotions, and expressing those emotions in movement. The combination may contain many positions that engage the eye of the viewer due to their freestyle look, but they are meaningless displays of ability unless emotion courses through the body while dancing them. Mattox always feels an emotion or a physical sensation while dancing, and this underlying meaning gives his combinations true artistic impact. No matter what individual jazz style he choreographs in, emotion and depth of feeling are what make the movement burst forth with meaning.

PERFECTION AS A GOAL

Studying freestyle jazz dance with Matt Mattox, for many dancers, can be summed up in one word – challenging. Mattox asks more of dancers than they have ever been asked before. His work demands skill in energy, polyrhythm, weight transfer, isolation, design awareness, and the ability of the dancer to access and express feelings. His movement phrases are demanding in their physicality and stamina, yet must be performed without undue muscle tension. Yet underneath all of this Mattox still asks for one more thing, that the dancer always approach his work with one desire – the desire to be perfect. The hunger to master all of the aspects of freestyle dance and to develop one's skills with the goal of arriving as a professional in the world of dance is necessary if the dancer is to achieve a successful career. Every moment that you dance, he says, you are sending a message to those who watch you about your ability and maturity as a participant in the dance community. The only way to excel and to present the best version of yourself is to always work towards perfection.

Considering the impressive stature of the workshops requesting

Mattox's classes, it is obvious that his technique is useful to ballet and modern dancers as well as jazz dancers. It is in demand by dancers of all levels of ability. In the professional world, some of his fans include Broadway director/choreographer Graciela Daniele, longtime Bob Fosse assistant Kathryn Doby, concert choreographer Margo Sappington, and modern dance legend Donald McKayle. Broadway choreographer Kathleen Marshall said in a recent article that today's dancers work on kicks and leaps, but fail to develop a knowledge of classic style and upper body sophistication. The Mattox freestyle jazz class develops Marshall's desired qualities.

The Mattox freestyle dance technique has been made available to all by producer Elizabeth Frich in *The Matt Mattox Book of Jazz Dance* and the accompanying videotape *Matt Mattox's JazzArt Technique*, but unfortunately they are out of print. Copies of these may be found in larger libraries. Only a few teachers in America are sanctioned by Mattox to teach his technique. Otherwise, dancers here must be content to wait for summer workshops when Mattox comes to the States. Thankfully Mattox has indicated that he intends to keep teaching as long as he can. He has pledged to continue to carry the torch and to enlighten new generations of dancers in the benefits and joys of his remarkable creation – freestyle jazz dance.

25
JACK COLE

by Bob Boross

Reprinted from *Jazzart* Jazz Dance Website, Copyright 2005

EARLY DANCE TRAINING

Jack Cole was born as John Ewing Richter in 1911 in New Brunswick, NJ, and spent his early years in Catholic schools and a military academy. It is felt that he developed a sense of inadequacy and a compulsive personality due to having a partially crossed eye, which was later corrected by surgery. Cole enrolled at Columbia University in New York, but soon left school to pursue a dance career after having witnessed a performance by the Denishawn dance company. He was taken in by Ruth St. Denis and Ted Shawn, and spent time learning and performing the pseudo-oriental movement repertory of the Denishawn troupe. Cole also performed with Doris Humphrey and Charles Weidman, and in Massachusetts with Ted Shawn's all-male dance company.

Cole was an unconventional young man, prone to dressing in unusual suits and moccasins and sporting a closely cropped hair cut. Cole held strong opinions on all forms of dance and art, and soon left the modern dance fold to find a living in commercial dance (remember, this was during the Depression). In a search for authenticity in East Indian dance, he studied with Uday Shankar and La Meri. He also made trips to Harlem's Savoy ballroom to watch the Lindy hoppers in action. He started doing niteclub work, performing with Alice Dudley and then Anna Austin and Florence Lessing. His work was a radical departure from the status quo in commercial dance. In a field where tap and jazzy routines dominated, where a chorus of pretty but non-trained dancers was the norm, Cole brought an intensely demanding and highly trained form of dance. He initially choreographed dances that were based on ethnic or exotic themes, and although he was snubbed by the dance establishment, Cole rapidly became a favorite of audiences in New York, Havana, and major cities across the U.S

THE FIRST THEATRICAL JAZZ DANCE STYLE

Cole's major accomplishment, according to published newspaper accounts, was first seen in a performance at the Rainbow Room night club in New York's Rockefeller Center on New Year's Eve, 1937. He had set the authentic movements of East Indian dances to the swing beat of jazz music. The rebounding feeling of the swing remarkably was a perfect match to the sharp, precise, isolated Indian movement. Audiences went wild over this dancing, and it was dubbed "Hindu Swing." Cole continued to add influences from jazz dancing and vernacular jazz dance movements, and he created a unique movement style. It wasn't pure Indian dance, or authentic jazz dance, or modern dance, yet it retained characteristic qualities of all three forms of dance. It was a style of dance, singular and instantly identifiable as "Cole." It was also the first formation of a theatrical jazz dance style that was suitable for the demands of artistic choreography.

The "Marriage of a Solid Sender" was a Cole jazz dance that appeared in the Broadway revue *Ziegfeld Follies* of 1943, and is considered by some to be the first successful artistic jazz dance. The bias towards the coverage of jazz dance by critics is evident in that relatively little has ever been written about this historic jazz dance. Or maybe they just had no idea of the impact this new style of dance would bring. As with most jazz and show dance, it only lives in the faded memories of those patrons lucky enough to have witnessed the performance. It is known, however, that a lindy step was the basis for the dance movement. Cole has also stated in interviews that, in his opinion, all theatrical jazz dancing is derived from the lindy.

As the reputation of Jack Cole as a niteclub performer and choreographer grew, so did the desire of the entertainment industry to make use of his talents. Cole spent the later 1940s and the 1950s bouncing back and forth between Broadway and Hollywood. He is credited with choreographing the Broadway shows *Magdalena*, *Carnival in Flanders*, *Kismet*, *A Funny Thing Happened On The Way To The Forum*, *Kean*, *Donneybrook!*, *Jamaica*, and *Man Of La Mancha*. His film work includes *Moon Over Miami*, *Cover Girl*, *The Merry Widow*, *Gentlemen Prefer Blondes*, *There's No Business Like Show Business*, *The I Don't Care Girl*, *Thrill Of Brazil*, *Down To Earth*, *Kismet*, *Les Girls*, and many more. And yet, having singlehandedly created the theatrical jazz dance idiom and being one of the most desired and prolific choreographers in film history, Jack Cole is still a forgotten legend, a cult hero known to a precious few.

LACK OF NOTORIETY

There are a few reasons for this, the most important being that Cole never had a big hit show. Jerome Robbins and Bob Fosse followed Cole, were influenced by Cole, but each had their own smash successes- Robbins' *West Side Story* and Fosse's multitude of dances that led up to *Sweet Charity*. We know who they are, but Cole never was associated with a successful show of that magnitude. Cole was also employed primarily as a choreographer, not a director/choreographer like the more well-known Fosse, Robbins, Gower Champion, and Michael Bennett. His only time as a director/choreographer was for *Kean* and *Donneybrook!*, both in 1961. And as for the world of concert dance, Cole preferred to present his work in niteclubs, where critics rarely came.

Another reason is that Cole's era in commercial dance overlapped the time of the highly popular but artistically opposite Florenz Ziegfeld and Busby Berkeley. Cole hit a brick wall in trying to get producers to change the status quo, to add dancing in unusual or innovative ways, or to experiment with camera angles and lighting. Being just a choreographer, producers interested in turning a buck were less likely to allow Cole to implement his ideas than someone like Gene Kelly, who had his star power to back up his innovative ideas on dance in film. A case in point- with many film producers the three areas of dance, sets, and costumes would not get together until the actual day of shooting, disallowing any creative synthesis between the various idioms.

Cole abhorred production strategies of this sort. While working on *Down To Earth*, Cole hired sketch artists to draw positions and formations of dancers and share this information with set and costume designers prior to shooting, so that a shared artistic vision could be forged.

Another reason for the lack of notoriety of Jack Cole to today's jazz dancer has to do with the changing nature of jazz dance itself. Cole's work was a highly disciplined and structured form of dance, performed to jazz or ethnic accompaniment. The advent of rock n roll in the 1950s and pop music of the 1960s changed the popular styles of dance and ushered in a new era of freedom in movement. Social dances of the 1960s had dancers who related more to the floor and themselves rather than their partners (like the lindy), and the beat didn't swing. As choreographers (like Fosse and Bennett) used the new music, show dancing changed and the Cole style dropped out of style. A new generation grew up not listening to swing music, watching old movies, or wanting to dance in such a structured fashion. And Matt Mattox, the popular jazz teacher most associated with the Cole style moved to London in 1970, breaking the continuum of the Cole lineage in America. The Cole era was lost, seen as a relic to be treasured only by those with the knowledge and appreciation of real jazz dance.

THE COLE STYLE

An interesting quote about Cole's personality, which aptly describes his movement style, was given by Hal Schaefer, Cole's longtime musical accompanist. In "Broadway - Remembering Jack Cole," Schaefer summed up Cole as uniquely being both "intellectual and savage." Cole used many ethnic and folk styles of dance (like East Indian, flamenco, and the lindy) as a source for movements, but used his knowledge of motivation for movement from his modern dance training to manipulate these sources into well-crafted choreographies. His style was derived from dance movements performed for centuries by common people, but theatricalized for use on the stage. This is why, when pressed for a definition of his movement, Cole termed it "urban folk dance."

When trying to describe Cole's movement, it is best to identify certain predominate characteristics. A partial list would include dancing in *plie*, with isolated body movements; with compressed or stored energy; and with a keen sense of manipulating rhythm, spatial levels, and attack. The first item of dancing in *plie* is a key to the Cole style, and one which is not seen often enough in today's dance world. Cole made great use of a wide and low second position, as well as a parallel fourth position with both knees bent and the back knee close to the floor. This wide stance dropped the dancer's center of gravity, and allowed the dancer to extend movement horizontally across the floor. This contrasted with the ballet dancer's vertical orientation. By using an ultra smooth transition of weight from foot to foot, a slinky, sensual feel was given by him and his dancers. Cole's movement is often called cat-like, or animalistic.

But while the weight center was dropped low to the floor, the torso remained very tall and erect. Cole's spine was lengthened and regal, giving a polished look. Even though his body was in *plie*, working with gravity, his torso at the same time defied gravity. This contradiction was magnified by his supple arms movements. Cole initiated arm movement from the center of the back, often involving the shoulder. This shoulder involvement in arm movement is characteristic of the way a cat will walk, adding to his reputation of having cat-like movement.

Isolation in body movement was another key to Cole's style. He made great use of side and forward thrust of the hips and shoulders, and even the head. Many of his isolations came from the tradition of East Indian dance. Cole used isolations to show rhythmic flow throughout the body, and to draw the attention of the audience to specific parts of the body.

MOVEMENT QUALITIES

Cole's dances generally had a consistent set of movement qualities. First was the used of recoil and release to launch bursts of energy. In a fashion similar to a cat crouching and compressing its hind legs in order to spring at its prey, Cole used his *plie* level in order to launch the body and give dynamic impact to his movements. Cole dancer Buzz Miller remembers him as being a "coiled spring."

Another quality was that of supreme strength in movement. His dancers were rock solid, and Graciela Daniele, the well-known choreographer and director of musicals at Lincoln Center, felt that Cole dancers were "warriors." An excellent description of this aspect of the Cole style was given by critic Debra Jowitt, who said "Cole dancing strikes me as immensely aggressive; almost every gesture is delivered with maximum force, but then has to be stopped cold in mid-air to achieve the clarity of design he wanted...an immense counter effort has to be used to stop the gesture."

Cole explored all spatial level in his choreography. Knee slides and floor work were common, and it was normal for dancers to spring from the deepest *plié* into high, suspended leaps. He also abhorred the smiling, happy face seen in most jazz and tap dance of the time. Instead, he preferred a cool, almost cold look in the eyes. He danced with a piercing gaze, much like a newly caged tiger, that could prod and intimidate an audience. Jazz teacher Nat Horne, who worked for both Jack Cole and Matt Mattox, noted this quality when he said that:

> *"Matt didn't like a lot of expression in class, and neither did Jack Cole. They liked that cool, cold look. But what often the student didn't understand was that even though they wanted that cool, cold look - underneath there was a fire in the center of the body, and the feeling of the shoulder isolation coming from the center. Sometimes the face would never change expression, but you could just see the body curl into the contraction."*

Rhythm is integral to Cole's style. Cole observed dancers at Harlem's Savoy Ballroom dancing the lindy, and utilized the swing feeling in their bodies. Swing music has a drop and recovery, much like a bouncing ball, that generates new energy on each rebound. This feeling, as transformed into authentic jazz dances, gives renewed energy and attack to each subsequent movement. Cole integrated this bounce and rebound into his movement, giving it a fresh and lively appearance. He also manipulated the dynamics of his movement, alternating passages of sharp attack with smooth, sinewy sections. This variation helped to give his choreography a spontaneous feel.

Cole's movement was so different from the standard styles of the time that the vast majority of dancers were not capable of executing it. So Cole also created his own dancers through classes and rehearsals. On the technical side, he devised a varied approach. Classes in Cechetti ballet were augmented by studies in East Indian dance, flamenco, ethnic dance, modern, and gymnastics. He wanted his dancers to be ready for any type of movement that he might devise. This movement was to performed flawlessly, so Cole demanded an intense focus on detail and precision. He is known for rehearsing his dancers for a full day on just eight bars of music, and there were times that he could not finish his dances in time for a show because the dancers could not meet his exacting standards. Gwen Verdon, in the New York Film Society of Lincoln Center's "Tribute to Jack Cole," said that "Jack once said to me 'I'm going to tell you what to do with the second joint of your little finger - so don't think that it's going to be any other way!'"

This relentless rehearsing honed his dancers to a razor sharp edge. It catapulted the dancers into another consciousness while performing. Critic John Martin said that a Cole dancer "is a depersonalized being, an intense kinetic entity rather than an individual. In this state of technical preparedness, which amounts to almost possession, he performs incredible movement, with a dynamism that transfers itself to the spectator as sheer motor enkindlement."

Another way Cole motivated his dancers was through suggestion. By outlining a clear understanding of the motivation for movement, he made his dancers move in a real and effective way. By giving visual images, sometimes graphic and shocking, to his dancers, he could coax them into fuller, more dynamic movement. Nat Horne remembered that:

> *"With the girls, he'd call them aside and say something in their ear, and when they came back they did it! And I have no idea, but I can imagine what sometimes he would say. Sometimes he would be very graphic with what he*

wanted you to think of. Sometimes you have to shock the students in a nice manner and give them images so the movement has meaning and not just technique behind them."

RELEVANCE TO TODAY'S DANCER

Next is the question of the value and relevance of Cole's technique and style to today's dancer. Can his methods help today's professional jazz dancer? Personally, I feel that a study of Cole's work will benefit not just jazz dancers, but all dancers. His work transcends jazz dance. It gives the dancers such precise and exacting control over their movements that they will be better at any technique. Cole's work brings clarity, strength, and very importantly, presence. These are qualities that any dancer will benefit from. Cole dancers command the eye of the audience, making the dancer a valued tool of the choreographer and therefore highly employable (just think of Gwen Verdon after she left Cole to work with Michael Kidd and Bob Fosse). As for jazz dance, Cole's application of motivation for movement brings the jazz dancer unarguably into the realm of artistic expression - something that jazz dance still is not known for. And if you are an aspiring Broadway and musical theatre dancer, knowledge of the Cole style will certainly enhance your success and employability.

Where can you find Cole training? Well, it's not easy. The most well known teacher using Cole influenced movement is Matt Mattox, who is highly regarded in France and throughout Europe, but no longer teaches. You might be able to catch some classes with former members of the American Dance Machine, a Broadway style dance company that put Cole's methods in the forefront of their training technique. Look for workshops with Ann Reinking, or in New York with Edmond Kresley at the American Musical and Dramatic Academy. Since Cole dancers are now older, it's best to ask senior teachers at conventions, schools, and universities. Or look for classes with Bob Boross in New York, who teaches the Mattox style and technique.

To read about Cole, try to find Glen Loney's *Unsung Genius: The Passion of Dancer - Choreographer Jack Cole.* It's out of print, but might be available in major libraries. Much of this book was excerpted in a ten part series in *Dance Magazine* in 1983. Theses have also been written on Cole. But the best place to get hooked on Cole is to watch his movies. Check out *Down to Earth* and *Tonight and Every Night* with Rita Hayworth, *Gentlemen Prefer Blondes* with Marilyn Monroe, and Monroe's "Havin a Heatwave" from *There's No Business Like Show Business.* Jack Cole is the prime innovator of our theatrical jazz dance heritage, and his work should be valued not only by jazz dancers, but by anyone seriously interested in dance as an art form.

26
LYNN SIMONSON

by Bob Boross

Reprinted from *Jazzart* Jazz Dance Website, Copyright 2005

The Jazz Dance Technique of Lynn Simsonson

In the mid 1960s, Lynn Simonson developed a jazz dance class in which the technique was independent of her style. Her approach was designed to develop the total dancer without the limitation of style, and was based on standards of kinesiology with respect to the individual's anatomical characteristics. In her determination to maintain a purity of technique, Simonson's style of movement was reflected only in her choreographed combinations. Simonson Jazz has endured the test of time as a fundamentally valid approach to a dancer's education. For over thirty years countless dancers around the world have passed through its training into the professional world.

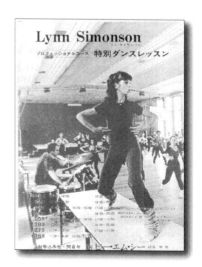

While many dance techniques demand that the dancer fit the ideal of the technique by forcing the body to accommodate positions and movement that may be inimical to its body mechanics, Simonson Jazz Dance is taught with the parameters of the individual dancer's body in mind - the natural range of motion that each individual has (i.e. what each individual dancer is capable of doing). A teacher of Simonson Jazz is trained to recognize work with musculoskeletal limitations in his or her students. Most dance injuries are due to faulty alignment or poor technique. Faulty alignment causes injury by placing stress on an area that wasn't designed to accommodate it. When alignment is poor, movement is inefficient, the body is fatigued, and injuries are caused; when alignment is correct, movement is efficient and injury free. Problems in technique can only be addressed after alignment has been corrected, since faulty alignment warps technique and inhibits the development of appropriate muscle groups.

A Description of a Simonson Jazz Dance Class

On December 20, 1996, I stopped in at the DanceSpace dance studio in lower Manhattan, NY, to observe Lynn Simonson teaching a jazz class. Although a brisk winter wind chilled the pedestrians outside on Broadway, the atmosphere inside was warm, cordial, and supportive.

Simonson is in her fifties, but she displayed the enthusiasm and love for dance of a young hopeful. She began her class with exercises that included rolling up and down, flat backs, and side stretches. The movements were executed in a slow, continuous fashion, without jerky or strenuous applications. Simonson repeatedly gave instructions on the proper execution of the exercises, and frequently used anatomical references to focus the attention of the students. Mentioned were the pubic bone, sitz bones, psoas  stretch, "lumbar spine moves forward as the sacrum moves back," and to "lift the sitz bones higher" in a forward stretch with straight legs.

The class continued on with rolling thru the feet, lunge and hamstring stretches, and then a *tendu* exercise that included a 1/4 *rond de jambe* and *demi plie*. During the exercises, Simonson used an entrancing tape of eastern sounding music, or drove the class with the aggressive rhythm she pounded on a hand drum. She walked constantly throughout the class, stopping to make individual corrections and noticing progress in students. Then came a series of *passe/ developpes* with flexed and pointed feet, to the front and back in parallel and turned out to the sides. This is followed by a set of releases and contractions, and a lunge stretch to the front with a torso twist, similar to the classic yoga stretch.

By this time, it is 30-40 minutes into the class, and Simonson asked the now perspiring students for an adagio that has been worked on previously in the week. Again, it is a smooth, fluid motion of contractions, lunges, torso spirals, *passe/ developpes*, and it included a brush back of the leg into an *arabesque* with an elongated body. The students work on the adagio in groups, and sit on the floor for stretches. The legs are straight in front, and they hold four counts with flexed and pointed feet in flat back and rounded positions. Floorwork continues with stretches in second position, and then with abdominal exercises. Simonson concludes the exercise portion of class by standing and executing a set of *battements*, in *attitude* with a pointed foot and then with a straight leg and a flexed foot, to the front and the sides.

The combination for the day is to a rhythmic drum selection by Cirque du Soleil. It is much like the exercises - smooth, fluid, lyrical - with contractions and a few sharper punches of the arms. In some ways, it reminds me of a jazzier version of some Horton technique movements. There is not much in the way of isolations, as the movement is sweeping and involves torso contractions rather than individual shoulder or hip isolations. It does include an *attitude* turn in plie than leads directly into a *developpe* front and a full body layout. There is also a *chaine* in *plie* into a split leap that descends to the floor. The combination is representative of a classical style of jazz dance - in *plie* with strong torso movements, but without the Broadway punch or flair of someone like Fosse or Cole. It does lean to modern dance, and it is easy to see why many Simonson dancers work successfully in modern dance companies.

The students range from obvious long time students of Simonson, to many new dancers here from Japan. The more accomplished ones exhibit a smooth flow of movement and a strong sense of where their center of strength comes from. A layman might say that they look really "together," meaning that there is no jerky or awkward movements. The upper level students are very confident in their projection, and they are "dancing" the combination rather than walking their way through it or just trying to remember it. When the most accomplished group dances, they are able to exhibit a sense of line, form, and spatial design. Placement is natural and without force, and the students are able to match the grandeur of the orchestral drum track with their emotional expression. Simonson urges them to be "influenced by the drum accents," and the students respond with willing faces.

The Simonson class was a well thought out approach to getting a body ready to dance, and, as evidenced by the positive outlook of the students, a jazz and modern dance style that allows for the dance expression and progression of any level dancer.

27
EUGENE LORING
AN UNSUNG INNOVATOR WHO FOUND
FREEDOM IN MOVEMENT

by Bob Boross

Reprinted from *Dance Teacher* magazine with permission, Copyright October 2006

Like the outlaw protagonist of his most famous ballet *Billy the Kid*, Eugene Loring (1911–1982) was a choreographer and teacher who wasn't afraid to cross boundaries. At a time when themes from European romantic ballet dominated the fledgling American ballet scene, Loring pioneered the "Americana" ballet trend of the 1930s by creating dances based on homegrown characters and by blending ballet vocabulary with elements of modern and folk dance. His signature *freestyle* training method—which synthesized movements and philosophies from jazz, ballet, modern, ethnic dance, and acting —was a pre-cursor to the more well known work of modern jazz innovators such as Jack Cole, Matt Mattox and Luigi. Loring's film choreography regularly challenged the status quo of showy tap and jazz routines with dances that displayed authenticity in style and adherence to plot and characterization. And his longstanding American School of Dance in Hollywood offered a curriculum, revolutionary at the time, that encouraged study in a variety of movement techniques.

Despite his many contributions as a dancer, choreographer and educator, Loring remains relatively unknown. His early career blossomed in the limelight of the New York City dance scene, choreographing for Ballet Caravan and dancing featured roles in works by George Balanchine, Michel Fokine and Agnes de Mille. But his move to the west coast to work in commercial films shrouded his achievements in relative obscurity. Through all of his work, however, Loring insisted that all dance forms have valid elements, and that

139

adherence to creating theatrical choreography that valued feeling in dance expression was preferred over the ornamentation and rigidity of old world dance pedagogic biases.

Born LeRoy Kerpestein in Milwaukee, Wisconsin, Loring studied acting as a teenager under Russian teacher Boris Glagolin and staged the dance sequences for his mentor's theatrical productions. The young Loring, armed with a letter of introduction to ballet patron Lincoln Kirstein given to him by a traveling actor, hitchhiked to New York and immediately began classes at the School of American Ballet, which Kirstein founded with Balanchine. He progressed swiftly, performing just months later in Balanchine's *Alma Mater, Reminiscence,* and *Card Party,* as well as in ballets by Fokine.

The late 1930s were a time of experimentation in American ballet, with some choreographers intent on replacing the aristocrats, peasants and sylphs of eighteenth-century European ballet with characters from the American landscape. Loring was a leading figure in this transformation of the art form, creating pieces such as *Yankee Clipper* (1937), *Billy the Kid* (1938) and *City Portrait* (1939) for Ballet Caravan, Kirstein's American touring company. It was *Billy the Kid,* Loring's homage to the wicked, misunderstood outlaw of American folklore that most notably set the course for the new trend of Americana ballet. Loring's ground-breaking work drew from movement sources outside of traditional ballet technique - modern dance, folk dance and acting characterization - to create something uniquely American. *Billy the Kid* predated other important American ballets, such as *Rodeo* (1941) by Agnes de Mille and *Fancy Free* (1944) by Jerome Robbins.

Loring's emerging philosophy of choreography drew from ideas pioneered by Jean-Georges Noverre and Fokine - that the components of dance should reflect the needs of the choreographic theme. He felt it was acceptable to make use of movements and styles outside of the boundaries of a particular dance technique, if it was the right or "truthful" choice to make the piece a successful whole. At a time when most choreographers insisted on the purity of their stylistic approaches, Loring experimented freely, creating pieces such as *The*

Great American Goof (1940), in which the performers recited text as they danced.

Loring continued to develop his philosophy of choreographic inclusion in 1941 with his newly formed company, Dance Players, whose company members included Lew Christensen, Michael Kidd, Janet Reed and Joan McCracken. Although it lasted for just one year, the company was an incubator for Loring's ideas, and in 1942 he created the critically acclaimed pieces *Prairie* and *The Man from Midian* - both based on American themes. Since Loring's movement style was radical for the time, a great deal of his energy went toward creating teaching methods to train his dancers, and it was here that he began in earnest to develop his freestyle approach.

In 1943 Loring cast his lot with the lure of Hollywood, where the demand for movement in films offered numerous opportunities for his unusual spectrum of talents. He was hired at age thirty-two by MGM with a previously unheard of six-part contract as a dancer, actor, choreographer, director, writer, and instructor. At a time when the film genre grossly appropriated ethnic dance forms as a means to create "exotic" appeal, Loring's presence on the Hollywood scene injected a fresh dose of authenticity in choreographic approach. Highlights of his film choreography include *Yolanda and the Thief* (1945) and *Ziegfeld Follies* (1946) starring Fred Astaire, *Deep in My Heart* (1954), *Silk Stockings* (1957) and the ballet sequences in *The Bandwagon* (1953) with Cyd Charisse. Some of Loring's most inventive film choreography can be seen in 1953's *The 5,000 Fingers of Dr. T,* based on the Dr. Seuss story.

Noting the inability of dancers trained in only one technique to pick up other movement styles, and determined to remedy it, Loring opened the American School of Dance in Hollywood in 1947. With classes in classical ballet, modern dance, tap, ethnic dance, choreography, dance history, dance on film, dance drawing, "Kinesiography" (Loring's own dance notation method), and early forms of theatrical jazz dance, the school's varied curriculum was unique among Los Angeles schools. Regardless of form, the goal of all the technique classes was the same: to stretch and strengthen muscles, define form and line, and enhance coordination.

Coinciding with the school's opening, Loring formalized a dance class called *freestyle*, which synthesized the most important elements of a variety of dance techniques into a single approach. It was a way to get dancers to break free of the restrictions of training in a single dance technique and make them more adaptable to the eclectic needs of film and theatrical choreography. The class featured floor and *barre* work, including many ballet exercises such as *plié*, *tendu* and *developpé* that were performed with a parallel hip alignment and renamed with a more American sounding terminology such as "descend," "leg brush" and "leg unfolding." Body isolations figured prominently in the class, as did improvisations drawn from acting techniques.

The freestyle class was the culmination of Loring's career and philosophy in dance: the elimination of boundaries and acceptance of all technical and stylistic forms, based on their merit. Freestyle broke ground for the emerging field of theatrical or "modern jazz" dance of the 1950s, and many of the pioneers in this field—including Cole, Mattox, Luigi, Gwen Verdon and Marie Bryant—were either students of Loring or invited teachers at the American School of Dance at that time. Freestyle was taught at the American School of Dance until it closed in 1974, and then at the University of California, Irvine, where Loring was the founding chair of the Department of Dance from 1965 to 1979.

Loring died in 1982, but his legacy lives on in *Billy the Kid* (which resides in the repertory of major ballet companies), in his film choreography, and in his lingering influence on the thousands of dancers who studied his methods at the American School of Dance and UC Irvine. His philosophy of fusing the most important qualities of multiple dance techniques into one method was a harbinger of the trend of the last fifty years to meld dance styles, blurring the boundaries between them. Although not generally acknowledged, Loring's influence on many dance forms, particularly theatrical jazz dance, is significant. His approach to dance was original, and his experiments yielded a technique that continues to give dancers the freedom to move in new ways.

28
THE JACK COLE SCRAPBOOKS
COLLECTION REVIEW

by Bob Boross

Dance Chronicle – Volume 27, Number 3, 2004. Copyright Bob Boross 2004

As important as Jack Cole was to twentieth-century commercial theatre dance, not enough substantive research has taken place on his career and achievements. There is the informative, yet uneven, biography *Unsung Genius – The Passion of Dancer-Choreographer Jack Cole* by Glenn Loney, as well as a few scholarly articles and master's degree theses, short articles for dance trade publications, and some articles by Cole himself. However, much of the information in these sources conflicts, as the authors have depended on the memory of those who worked with Cole. Often the information is incorrect because of Cole himself - he was known to have enjoyed telling a good story and the embellishments added each time he recounted an experience in his life make for multiple versions of the truth. For these reasons, and considering the magnitude of his dance output and the extraordinary range of influences in his work, a biography of Jack Cole could stifle even the best researcher.

That is why information collated by Cole himself, in the form of five scrapbooks held by the Theatre Museum in London, in Covent Garden, is so important in trying to understand the driving force behind his work. During his career, Cole kept large scrapbooks filled with programs, reviews, newspaper clippings, photos, and other memorabilia of his work. Originally Cole had seven scrapbooks, but only five contained mounted material, and at his death in 1974 two remained stuffed with loose clippings, which have been removed and boxed. Along with Cole's vast library of dance books, costumes, and memorabilia, his belongings were auctioned off in 1979 in London, with most disseminated into private collections and museums. But the scrapbooks remained together and are now owned by the Theatre Museum. Although the first book is called "How It All Began" and inscribed with the date 1930, the earliest item is a 1913 photo of Cole's mother and a young child, assumed to be Cole. Throughout the scrapbooks Cole's life as a dancer and choreographer is revealed, from his early association with Ruth St. Denis and Ted Shawn, Doris Humphrey and Charles Weidman, to his nightclub acts and his juggling of work in Hollywood films and Broadway shows.

On a basic level, the collection would be of interest to researchers of early modern dance in America, as there are photos, programs, and reviews of many 1930s Denishawn performances, along with candid photos of Ruth St. Denis with her nephews, Doris Humphrey and Charles Weidman in embrace, and Ted Shawn posed as a powdered white statue. Cole saved many letters from Shawn, in which Shawn admonished the young Cole for his chronic lateness and recalcitrance - traits ironically that Cole would have never accepted in his own behavior or that of others in his later career. Shawn's early Jacob's Pillow retreats and men's dance group are well represented. Others captured in photos from those days are Ada Korvin, Marcus Blechman, Letitia Ide, Alice Dudley, Florence Lessing, Anna Austin, Barton Mumaw, Campbell Griggs, and even a young José Limón. In a later era, many photos document Cole's choreographic relationship with the ill-fated Marilyn Monroe.

Scholars of jazz dance history will find newspaper ads, reviews, and photo clippings of Cole and his partners during the nightclub era, but they will be frustrated by Cole's failure to include any information about the name of the newspaper and sometimes even the reviewer.

Nevertheless, much factual information can be gleaned from the text. For example, Cole's first performance of his "Hindu Swing" pairing of East Indian dance and swing music was on December 31, 1937, at the Rainbow Room in New York City's Rockefeller Center. This directly contradicts an account given in Loney's biography in which Florence Lessing states that this occurred in 1942 at the suggestion of the dancer-photographer Marcus Blechman. Also there is revealing information about the role the Rainbow Room played, at the direction of the room's booking manager John Roy, in replacing staid supper-club entertainment with the work of concert dancers like Agnes de Mille, Paul Draper, Helen Tamiris, Monna Montes, and Cole. But disappointingly little is available in terms of photos of Cole's early jazz dance work that might add to the knowledge of what his early jazz work looked like, particularly the seminal "Marriage of a Solid Sender" dance performed by Cole in 1941. (In all references in the scrapbooks, this piece is referred to as "Marriage of a Solid Sender," rather than "Wedding of a Solid Sender" as reported in Loney's book and other scholarly articles.) Historians searching for more detail concerning Cole's actual movement will have to look elsewhere.

The scrapbooks, however, prove a treasure trove of information on Cole's psyche, since he assembled page after page of nude and semi-nude photos of himself, and created homoerotic art and collages that imply his coming to terms with his homosexuality – remarkably, an all-important aspect not discussed in Loney's book. It is known that Cole suffered from an unhappy childhood, with time spent in a military academy and an accident that left him with a cast in one eye, and it has been theorized that these contributed to his violent, repressed nature. However, the scrapbooks indicate that from his early years Cole was questioning his sexual preference, which could have been a stronger contributing factor to his personality. He reputedly married in the 1930s and had a son, but about 1937 he established a relationship with the actor David Gray, which they maintained until Cole's death. Cole went through a dark period in 1948, in which he created a scrapbook page filled with shadowy headshots of himself in various states of tortured despair, all framed with black cloth gaffer's tape – quite a foreboding sight. A hand drawn sign proclaims that it was "A Time of Great Emotional Stress." But his entries following this time indicate a change in his demeanor.

Cole was the subject of a 1950 photo-laden *Dance Magazine* article, which he embellished with drawings and cryptic collages and proclamations. It seems to be his coming-out, a veiled expression of his acceptance of his sexual preference. Although he had choreographed many Betty Grable films, Cole railed at the top of the article that he had no desire to "dance" with Betty Grable, "no matter how attractive she is." Instead, in the photos he portrays himself as a harlequin who wants "to be a sort of 'eternal clown,' being comic, sad, or gay to any audience, anywhere." In the article, hidden messages emerge. As the clown, he was on a journey set by Fate (played in the photos by Gwen Verdon). He remarked, "If I can really become Harlequin the Clown, I can speak to people any place in the world and be understood." At the completion of his journey, Cole, after being "cheated by Fate," contemplates the "patterns of nature."

Another strong clue can be found in many seminude photos of Cole in which his forearms and tightly clenched fists are wrapped in strips of a beige material. At first look Cole, wearing only a G-string or tight shorts and standing fiercely with forearm and fist thrusting vertically to the sky at shoulder level or reclining with he forearm strategically projecting from his hip area, gives off the masculine aura of a gladiator. However, inscribed within these photos in a hand drawing that Cole made of a similar forearm/fist wrapped in strips of fabric. Here, with Cole's added emphasis, it can be seen that the wrapped forearm/fist is actually meant to be a phallic image. On this same page Cole also assembled a series of photos of a curiously opened hand, fingers together but thumb released giving a vulnerable look. The hands are linked in a linear progression by drawn arrows, and with each photo in the series the hand becomes larger, as if growing in age. The final photo is of a hand delicately holding a white flower in its fingertips.

Considering Cole's photography and statements along with this underlying homoerotic expression, it is obvious that his work needs to be evaluated in a new light. Rather than focusing on his movement creation of a modern jazz dance style and technique, and his noted temper and drive for perfection, Coles' work is ripe to be analyzed for hidden sexual content and ways in which he could be proclaiming his sexuality through his choreography. The strong and forceful thrusting movements of his dances may now be seen as having a different motivation. Cole's work was always considered to be sexual in nature (it was often censored or toned down from its original versions). But his film choreography, particularly after this 1950 breakthrough, can now be seen to laden with hidden expressions of his homosexuality and sexual fervor.

Cole was not able to live openly as a gay man in the 1950s. In his film appearance as the flamboyant choreographer Randy Owens in *Designing Women* (1957), Cole had to fend off Gregory Peck's inference that he was "less than a man" with the offer to "beat both of your [Peck's] ears off" while producing photos of his character's wife and three strapping sons. Yet Cole did aspire to a typically normal American life, as his scrapbooks contain photos of conventional American bliss - walking his cocker spaniels, sunbathing at his Hollywood Hills home, and deep in contemplative research within his book-lined library. He was not able to say openly who he was in real life, but he was able to express aspects of his personality in his movement and choreographic inventions. A willing dance public and American audience accepted and praised Cole's work, yet that same public and audience could not rationalize the forces that created his thrilling work. Perhaps this is where the real Jack Cole lies - not in his "Hindu Swing" (which he labels in a scrapbook interview as "parlour entertainment" and as something on which to be "cashed in") or his first innovation of melding modern, East Indian, and jazz dance into an artistically synthetic jazz dance style, but rather in his inner conflict over his sexuality, his coming to terms with it, and his subsequent expression of that aspect of himself in his movement and work. Who is Jack Cole? With the help of his own scrapbooks, perhaps his true nature can now be deduced.

29
EMPTY SKY...THE RISING
A RESPONSE TO CATASTROPHE THROUGH DANCE

by Bob Boross

Glory Days: A Bruce Springsteen Symposium – September 2005

Copyright Bob Boross 2005

I am a dance choreographer, and my work involves the creation of characters that express stories, ideas, and emotions through choreographed dance movement. On September 7, 2005, I premiered my evening length piece, *Empty Sky...The Rising*, at the Two River Theater in Red Bank, NJ. In this piece I choreographed dance and acting movement to illustrate the hardships endured by many people as a result of the catastrophic events of the collapse of the twin towers of New York's World Trade Center on September 11, 2001. My inspiration for this piece was the music of Bruce Springsteen, both from his 2002 CD *The Rising* and his song *Land of Hope and Dreams*.

The creation of this piece required a collaborative, conceptual partnership between myself and the existing Springsteen lyrics and music. I chose eleven songs from *The Rising's* fifteen songs (making a total of twelve songs in the piece), and each song was unique in its examination of the thoughts, emotions, and characterization of ordinary people challenged by this extraordinary event. For me to illustrate these characters through theatrical dance movement, I needed to not only try to understand the given aspects of Springsteen's stories and people (time, place, name, gender, emotional motivation, etc), but also to allow my own creativity to build on Springsteen's basis. In my choreographic journey I found ways of inventing my own characters and inserting them into the story line, or of changing the order of songs from the original *Rising* line up, thereby finding new relationships between characters and songs. Bruce Springsteen wrote *The Rising* collection with his ideas in mind, and what I did was to take many aspects of his ideas and add my ideas, or in some cases to entirely supplant his ideas with mine.

Which is not to say that Springsteen was entirely not involved in my process. To secure the stage performing rights to his music, I first created a workshop version of ten of the songs in November 2003. A DVD of this workshop was sent to his management company with a request for performance use the music, and eventually Springsteen examined and approved my interpretation of his music. Since his management had explained to me that in the past  he had pulled his music from outside uses that he felt were not in keeping with his conceptual intent, I have to conclude that by giving his permission, Springsteen at some level was amenable to my concepts for his music, as shown in my dance movement.

In this paper I will discuss my experiences in this "one way" conceptual partnership, and also my challenges in adapting my knowledge of dance composition to the specific limitations and personality of rock music, which is not arranged for dance composition. I will also examine how I adapted to working with Springsteen's very powerful lyrics (many dance choreographers will shy away from music with lyrics and instead prefer instrumental songs). But first, I will give a quick statement as to my personal dance experience and heritage, as my "tools of the trade" have uniquely affected and guided my method of approach and choreographic process.

My background in dance is varied, and I have studied ballet, jazz dance, modern dance, tap dance, and musical theatre dance styles, as well as acting and dramatic direction. Having grown up listening to popular music on the radio since the 1960s, and having been influenced by the classic movie musicals of the 1940s and 50s, I bring an eclectic skill set to any project that I approach. I bring an "everyman" personality to my work. This differs from some dance approaches, as in serious classical ballet, for instance, where a dancer will religiously study only structured, formal ballet technique, or in some forms of modern dance, where dancers are known to follow the styles of individual choreographers like Martha Graham, Merce Cunningham, or other post modern choreographers. Dancers like these, although they are very strongly trained in their particular areas, tend to be limited to only these areas. Since they quite often are dancing onstage strictly as bodies moving in space, they do not emulate real people or real emotions.

My work is in opposition to this approach. My heritage first goes back to my primary influence, the teacher/choreographer/performer Matt Mattox. He was a star of the dance musicals of the 1940s and 50s, and subsequently created a dance technique and style called "freestyle," meaning that the dancer is skilled in many forms and styles of dance, and that he is free to choose from any of these forms or a mixture of forms when creating movement for a unique choreographic project. Mattox was influenced by the choreographers Jack Cole, and Eugene Loring, both known for their eclectic work in films, Broadway, and dance companies from the 1930s to the 1960s. They all made great use of acting techniques, and motivation for movement in the creation of their dances. Their initial forays into the freestyle dance philosophy led to Mattox's work starting in the 1950s. I have been similarly trained, and I use this approach whenever I begin to choreograph a new piece.

Empty Sky...The Rising

The Springsteen songs I chose for this piece, performed in this order, were: *Empty Sky, Lonesome Day, Nothing Man, Into the Fire, The Fuse, Mary's Place, You're Missing, Waitin' on a Sunny Day, Paradise, My City of Ruins, The Rising,* and *Land of Hope and Dreams.* I found a natural starting point for the piece with *Empty Sky,* a song that allowed me to introduce the event that spawned the challenges to the characters. It also allowed me to introduce many of the characters in short phrasings of dance movement. By doing this, the audience would be familiar with the characters, and ready to absorb their particular stories as they emerged in later songs.

Also, with this order of songs I was able to establish a narrative thread through the entire piece – first the introduction of the events and the main characters, then the exposition of each character's challenges in each song, and then a transition to a storyline in the final three songs that addressed the emotions felt universally by all people. This culminated in the presentation of a moral, or direction, as a way to deal with the challenges and the grief. Although Springsteen wrote about all of these challenges, and did offer the direction that I eventually took up, the arrangement of songs that I created enhanced some of Springsteen's aspects, and revealed new insights. For instance, the trio of *The Fuse, Mary's Place,* and *You're Missing* became the tragic story of two young lovers - their meeting and courtship, her loss as he is taken from her at an early age, her conflicting struggle as to how she can find the joy to freely dance again after having experienced such pain, and a look into her future of dealing with the pain of losing a lover and how she can live within a society where many have never experienced that pain.

A similar trilogy is *Paradise, My City of Ruins,* and *The Rising,* where I have created a suicide bomber, the bomber's mother as a religious zealot, everyday people shopping and strolling, and a dancer as a symbol of the mothers of all of all the characters who had dropped to the floor in mangled body positions at the explosion of the bomb. These dancers then turn to face a symbol of all people who died in the 9/11 event. When they attempt to resuscitate this symbol, their failure leads to a voice from the heavens explaining to the spiritual character that the only way to deal with the loss is to send their souls to their spiritual land. This happens in the tribal outpouring of *The Rising,* and finally a re-uniting with lost loved ones in *Land of Hope and Dreams.*

Creating an evening length piece to such a specific event and lyrical component required that I be fully in sync with Springsteen's method of writing and composition. In many ways Springsteen and I are quite alike – I grew up in central NJ, just minutes from his hometown of Freehold; I came from a working class family and spent many happy summer days in the arcades of Asbury Park; and I can surely identify with Springsteen's stated social status of always "being on the outside,

looking in." And I did find a release in the rock and soul music of the 1960s and 70s. When I first heard Springsteen's album *The Wild, The Innocent, and the E Street Shuffle* in 1974, I was instantly drawn to his lyric approach, subject matter, and his rhythmic patterns and sounds. His emotions were also mine, and since then I have always felt at one with his music. Perhaps this common heritage has enabled me to pull so much out of his music. Perhaps this one way relationship of listening to his music over a thirty year period, with Springsteen being the originator and myself being the listener - always reacting to his stories - has honed my skill in allowing his music to let my imagination soar.

This dates back to the summer of 1980, when I debuted a choreographic version of his classic song, *Jungleland*. At that early time in my dance career, I was enamored with the gang characters of the musical *West Side Story*. In *Jungleland*, I was able to pull from this Broadway musical dance heritage, to choreograph the story of a gang member who longs for escape from his environment, only to have the other inhabitants refuse his desire and to crush his dream. Springsteen's music has always spoken to me in visual images, and *Jungleland* was an early example of that.

A necessary skill for a good musical theatre choreographer is to be able to pick up on the emotions hidden in music, not only through the lyrics, but also in the melody, rhythm, and overall feel of the music. This is a skill that was of great advantage to me in forming the concepts for this piece. I choreograph not as other choreographers do - by experimenting in the studio in free improvisations - but by listening to the music and *imagining*. With *The Rising*, I created the concepts and choreographic formats by listening to the songs with headphones, preferably in a slightly darkened room and with no other stimuli to divert my attention. I listen, let the music take over my mind, and just imagine. Sometimes lyrics will make a movement or pose dart into my mind, while often the rhythm and emotional feel of the music will do just the same. I will get ideas as to movement patterns on stage, gestures, opening or ending poses, and more. This is how I created *ESTR*. Over a ten-day period, I listened to one song per day, and mapped out the concept and choreographic structure of each song.

I'd like to digress for a moment, and relate this method of choreographic creation to the freestyle heritage. In freestyle, a dancer or choreographer trains religiously in various dance forms, creating a body instrument that is able to execute any movement demand made upon it. But in choreography, the freestyle dancer relies a great deal on instinct, or that instantaneous reaction known as "reflex." When the mind reacts instinctively, with a reflex action, the body follows with a movement that is "true" since it is the natural, unaffected reaction to a stimulus. The past experiences of the artist make up the background upon which the decision is made, but the decision, being made without undue thought or consideration is the right and proper decision. It is the truth, and therefore entirely valid. This is how I created the entire *ESTR* piece - just listening and reacting, and using my background in many forms of dance as a basis for my instinctual decisions. I didn't make active decisions to impress a certain style of movement or composition on the piece. I just took what came as I listened in the darkness. This method served to make Springsteen's music the sole catalyst for my ideas, and cemented our unique creative partnership.

Creating the full *ESTR* piece involved a tremendous amount of conceptual thought, much more than can be explained in the time limitations of a presentation such as this. To illuminate my process and partnership with Springsteen, and its effect on the piece, I would like to give a fuller explanation of two conceptual decisions that resulted in specific theatrical staging ideas - ideas that are central to the piece.

Lonesome Day

In the song *Lonesome Day*, Springsteen sings about the character's shaken faith in the higher spiritual word, and how this event has challenged his belief in the higher word.

> *Baby once I thought I knew, everything I needed to know about you. Your sweet whisper, your tender touch. I really didn't know that much. The joke's on me, but I'm gonna find my way... after this lonesome day.*

Now, this statement could be attributed to just about any person living through the terror of that day. But for me, the challenge was how to use this declaration in service of the entire piece. Again, it came upon me instinctively, by allowing myself to be open and ready for a thought to enter - to make the character dancing this stanza not just an average person, but a preacher, or a spiritual person. This allowed me to create a more interesting double dilemma for this character and the song – the preacher is responsible for urging his people to maintain their faith by believing in the word, yet the preacher's faith is challenged due to those very same questions. He must tell his people that "It's all right, it's all right" yet he periodically looks up to the heavens with the same questions that his people have. By taking Springsteen's lyrics and intent, and then adding my own interpretation in service of my idea and need for this character later in the piece, I was able to lay the groundwork for a central concept of the piece - that our faith will repeatedly be challenged in extraordinary ways. I choreographed this lyric phrase as the preacher speaking to God, establishing a dialogue between the preacher and God, and this idea would used again much later on in the piece. I gave the preacher the role of being a leader of spiritual salvation for the rest of the dance characters. And by having a dual dilemma, it made for an opening dance song that was rich in underlying dramatic textures as well as being dynamic in performance values. The thought that flashed into my mind – to make the *Lonesome Day* primary character a preacher or spiritual person – was one of the first building blocks of the entire piece.

Empty Sky

A second major recurring concept is the dual nature assigned to the image of the "empty sky" in the song *Empty Sky*. Upon first listening, Springsteen's phrase seems to refer to the empty sky of the New York City skyline the day after the collapse (*"Empty sky, empty sky, I woke up this morning to an empty sky."*) The association of the "empty sky" to the physical is an obvious deduction. But it also came to me that the empty sky could also refer not just to the empty skyline that we all share, but to our unique personal emptiness that we all felt in some manner after the tragedy.

I woke up this morning, I couldn't barely breathe. Just an empty impression in the bed where you used to be...I woke up this morning to an empty sky.

The mention of the lingering impression in the bed made by the singer's lover - now to remain forever empty - pointed me towards creating a sub plot for the entire piece about personal emptiness as opposed to the geographic emptiness of the collapsed buildings. My decision next was to employ a theatrical device of making an illumination of the empty impression through stage lighting. The swath of light projected next to the character as she slumped on the floor allowed the character to interact with the empty impression, to see where it was, but also to allow for her hands to pass through the light. It was a perfect theatrical vehicle for getting across the idea of the empty impression, and the idea that the memory is there, but not actually tangible. We see and feel the light, or the memory, but we can no longer physically touch it and possess it.

This idea to contrast the personal and collective empty sky, or perhaps also explained as emotional and geographic empty sky, became

a repeated device during the piece. As this leading female character would return in the middle and end of the piece, she would use the swath of light as a place to express her deepest feelings, and to maintain a dialogue with the missing person. It returned in *Mary's Place*, where she talks to him (the swath of light), then tries to find a way to dance freely in spite of the new pain that she carries. She returns to it in mid-song, with another conversation, and a reach into the light with her hand that results in her feeling his heartbeat still in the empty space (the beat she displays with her hand is also the thump-thump of Garry Tallent's bass line in the song – the rhythmic backbone of the rock beat). Finally, after she does find a moment in which she can finally let herself go, the party ends and she is left expended, and still facing the emptiness and the empty impression. She falls to the floor and collapses as her hand reaches into the light in despair.

This light representing the empty personal sky is reprised in *You're Missing*, and also at the conclusion of *The Rising*, when after all the characters join force to send the lost souls on to their spiritual destiny, she returns to the light, as she did in *Empty Sky* and *Mary's Place*, and grieves as she slips her hand into the empty impression. It is both warm, due to the light, yet cold, due to its emptiness. It reflects her destiny -

that while here on earth, she will always remember the good times but be destined to live daily with the inescapable loss of her loved one. This aspect of the "empty sky" is more compelling and poignant than the geographic aspect. It tugs harder at our emotional strings, and made for a clever and valuable theatrical tool in developing the exploration of the Springsteen song *Empty Sky*.

These two instances give a strong idea of how I worked with Springsteen's lyrics - taking his ideas and either representing them as given or spinning them off in the service of my own interpretation or in the needs of the dramatic and narrative thread of the piece. From the preacher of *Lonesome Day* to the empty swath of light in *Empty Sky*, the symbolic mother of the victims of the suicide bomber in *Paradise* to the collective sympathy exhibited by the friends and relatives of mourners in *Into the Fire*, and the marching, automaton figures of *The Fuse* who represent a funeral procession, a slowly ticking clock, and a burning fuse that steadily moves towards it explosive destiny - the lyrics of Bruce Springsteen's *The Rising* collection served as an imaginative stimulus and conceptual basis for my own interpretation of his work and the September 11 event.

Methods of Choreographic Composition

Choreographing artistic dance movement is a highly personal act. Although many standard ideas like grouping movement in short phrases, using canon patterns, establishing solo and group patterns, etc, are used by all choreographers, most tend to develop their own approaches based on years of experience and the particular needs of the piece. My approach to *ESTR* fits this description, although my work here shifts strongly into dramatic characterization and storytelling. The utilization of acting methods was just as prominent in my mind as methods of dance composition. As one dancer in the 2003 workshop once related to me, "This piece seems like one big acting exercise!"

I would like to discuss some unique methods that I applied to specific songs, but first let me talk about the overall movement style of the piece. In *The Rising* CD, Springsteen sings about people who have strong thoughts and therefore strong motivations. For instance, from *Nothing Man*:

You want courage, I'll show you courage you can understand. The pearl and silver resting on my night table, Its just me Lord, I pray that I'm able...

In this song, a reluctant hero wrestles with the adulation of the public due to his actions in saving lives on 9/11, yet he feels that he did not do anything special to deserve such focused attention. He reacted instinctively, in the heat of the moment, and cannot rectify this special attention with the large-scale suffering that has occurred. The character of the Nothing Man flirts with taking his own life. He is feeling sharp and conflicting emotions, and from an acting standpoint, has tremendous motivation for his movements.

To adequately express the Nothing Man's extraordinary emotional challenge, dance movement from the fields of ballet and modern dance are not entirely suitable - in that they are concerned more with creating pleasing body lines or abstraction to express ideas - and not a specific person, time, or place. My task was to create movement that melded the locomotor aspects of more formal dance techniques with the expressive aspect of specific gestures. An example can be seen in the his movement that accompanies Springsteen's lyric "*I am the Nothing Man.*" During the musical point where Springsteen sings this phrase, I placed the character directly facing his wife, with the result that this simple sentence became a soul searching, revealing declaration of his emptiness, his pain, and his destiny. The dancer who portrays the Nothing Man executes the more standard dance movements called a pirouette (a spin of the body), a contraction (a tightening of the abdominal muscles), and an opening of his arms to his wife in an admonition of his situation. But in order to highlight his emotional state, I also grafted onto these generic movements a shameful turn of the head to the side as he executed the contraction and pirouette, and a tight clench of the torso and neck and arms as he begins his admonition, and finally a release to a flaccid muscle state of the torso to reflect his dual inner thought of his extreme pain and his method of dealing with that pain by assuming the stance of feeling nothing. There is a conscious application of gesture and body positions generated by the expression of emotional states to the locomotor movements found in formal dance techniques. This method of grafting motivation for movement, emotional expression through gesture, and the manipulation of tension and release within the body to the standard dance locomotor movements allowed me to create a movement style that was suitable for expressing the emotional states of each character, and also to help tell and further the story line of each song.

As you may deduce, this meant that each song and its narrative had to be scrutinized as if it were a play. Motivations, needs, and desires for each character were examined and discussed with the dancers, and the "why" of each movement was just as important as the resulting movement itself. By understanding the reason why a movement was executed, the decision as to the final choice of the movement and the way it was eventually executed became very particular. Dancers rehearsed incessantly to find the exact way to touch a partner, tilt the head, and look to the horizon. Often, my corrections and direction to them dealt more with what they were thinking as they executed the movement, rather than the movement itself. If the dancer truly felt the motivation, then the resulting movement became more real. As with the aforementioned tenant of freestyle dance, the use of instinctual or reflex action - in this case with movement that was generated by a pure and unaffected thought resulted in the proper movement to express that idea or emotion.

Aside from the general movement style of the piece, I applied a few specific methods of composition that drew from concert dance and also from acting techniques to dance composition. These methods, for the most part, dealt with some form of manipulation of the passage of time. The actual tragic event of 9/11 played out within a matter of hours. Yet millions of people watched and participated as observers of the event. This means that, if you consider each individual participation and reaction, there would be literally millions of hours of unique experience of the 9/11 event. In order to examine a few of the personal hardships, as sung by Springsteen and in my theatrical manifestation, it became necessary to replay the flow of time for each character, to consider their circumstances during the time period of the actual 9/11 event. I will now discuss a few of the methods by which I manipulated time frames, in order to highlight the individual experience, which were used to create my staging for the songs *Empty Sky, Mary's Place*, and *You're Missing*.

Empty Sky / Post-Modern Dance

Up to the mid-twentieth century, a dance was always considered to take place in a particular space and within certain duration of time. During the 1960s and 70s, a group of radical choreographers challenged that idea, experimenting with manipulations of these two concepts and creating artificial realities. This movement has been labeled as "post-modern" dance, in that the ideas advanced by these choreographers were breaking the mold established by the more structurally ordered modern dance choreographers of the 1940s and 50s time period. One such post-modern choreographer is Twyla Tharp. Although she is currently recognized for her more commercial work with the Broadway show *Movin' Out*, set to music by Billy Joel, her early work in the 1960s reflected a great deal of experimentation in dance composition.

In her 1970 piece titled "The One Hundreds," Tharp taught short movement phrases to one hundred dancers (on some occasions this piece was performed by normal people not trained in dance). First the movements were performed in consecutive sequence by the one hundred dancers, taking a considerable amount of time to do so. Then, the movements were performed simultaneously by all one hundred dancers, resulting in a short burst of energy enhanced by the reduced length of time. Her dual experiment allowed the audience either to see and study the individual movements as it was performed sequentially, or to revel in the myriad activity of a short burst of manic energy as the movement was performed simultaneously.

My staging of *Empty Sky* drew from this manipulation of time and space - I repeatedly accentuated intense bursts of emotional energy felt by the characters. As stated earlier, I used this piece as an introduction to characters that would be seen in more detail in later songs. My decision here was to give the dancers - two or three from each upcoming song for a full total of ten dancers - a short nine-count movement phrase from their song that summed up their personality and challenge. Then, I manipulated their execution of these movements - either performing them simultaneously to accentuate the intensity of the emotions spawned by their predicaments, or in sequence, so that each movement phrase and emotion could be examined in more detail.

The idea also came from another source - watching video clips on television of the same tragic moment on television. During those days of 9/11, we watched the same video clip of the planes crash into the towers repeatedly, or of the smoke cloud billowing down the streets of lower Manhattan as people fled in terror and vanished as they were engulfed. This idea of being subjected repeatedly to a singular emotional experience, through technology, was what I wanted to reflect in the compositional method. The characters tumbled forward in their short emotional movement phrase, and then quickly and calmly reassembled at the rear of the stage - only to break into the emotional phrase and move down to the audience over and over again. My choreography was like watching a video clip, hitting the rewind button, and then watching it over and over again.

This method of composition worked well with Springsteen's musical structure, and dynamic delivery of emotions. As he would sing *"Empty sky, empty sky, I woke up this morning to an empty sky"* over and over, it seemed to me like a replaying video clip. It was the same message - so short yet so astounding that it needed to be repeated endlessly in order for us to attempt to comprehend it. Each time he repeated the phrase, he added a higher emotional pitch, or the musical orchestration added more intense sounds. The effect of Springsteen's choice in lyrics, delivery, dynamics, and orchestration was to pound the exasperating and incredulous nature of the event into our minds, whether it is with the voice of someone who cannot fathom the event, or is raging at the fact that it did actually happen. Again, referring to my freestyle approach and my past experience with many concert dance methods of expression, I just listened to Springsteen, tried to pick up on the emotions and thoughts that he was expressing, and a suitable method for displaying my reaction in dance movement emerged.

Mary's Place and Stop-time

Time again was manipulated in the song *Mary's Place*. Bruce sings:

I've got seven pictures of Buddha, the prophet's on my tongue, eleven angels of mercy sighing over that black hole in the sun. My heart's dark but its rising, I'm pulling all the faith I can see, from that black hole on the horizon, I hear your voice calling me. Let it rain, let it rain, let it rain, let it rain, let it rain, let it rain, let it rain...Meet me at Mary's Place.

My reaction to this opening phrase of lyrics was to see two different worlds – the personal that we carry around with us, hidden,

every day – and the communal (Mary's Place), where we all meet and interact. He sang both of the character's personal thoughts and the idea of going to a location to socialize with others and participate in a group reality. These two sets of feelings and interactions take place simultaneously, but in order to examine each one more deeply, I felt a need to create two separate time sets - as Springsteen did lyrically - to show the multitude of emotional thoughts that occur within the same period of time. Throughout the song, Springsteen's musical structure alternated between the group reality of the party location of Mary's Place, and the inner thoughts of the character as she made her way through this party. It was easy for me to create both realities in consecutive time frames, rather than in simultaneous time frames, and with the aid of the previously mentioned swath of light that represented the lost lover.

Since the character's inner thoughts were mostly a dialogue with the lost lover, she begins the song in a personal communication with the swath of light in the most personal area of the stage – downstage center. From there, she makes her way upstage to enter and participate in the party of Mary's house. As the party swells and progresses, she makes her way back down stage to her personal space to reveal her inner thoughts once more. Eventually, near the center of the song, she actually "stops" time. With a wave of her hand, her building emotional conflict fuels her desire to speak to her missing lover once more, and the party dancers freeze in mid-motion. She has frozen time, in order to take time to examine her emotions, make her plea to her lost one, and to find a bit of him deep in her so that she can once again find the joy to dance. Once this has occurred, she then slowly begins to work into the dance movement of the dancers at Mary's Place, and back up stage into their world. Slowly the dancers come back to life as their time is re-ignited. The two time periods become one - simultaneous - and she dances furiously and joyfully with them. By using this stop-time method, I was able to illustrate the relation of her personal emotional process to the activities of the group, and subsequently lead to the resolution of the song. I was also able to follow the musical and contextual path set by Springsteen with his lyrics and story, and match my movement to his song.

You're Missing and Dual time frames/personalities

Staging Springsteen's *You're Missing* was a formidable task. His music is direct, yet incredibly evocative and poignant. He creates strong visual images and particular locations. This is the type of song that many choreographers shy away from staging, as it is difficult to establish a link to the music and theme without overtly imitating it. My decision here was to still work closely with the location and characters that Springsteen gives in the song, but then to embellish my interpretation through the use of a "dual time frame and personality." As before, I used a technique from the world of acting to create a more varied and rich approach to the song than would be found if one was just reacting to the music as written.

In the song, Springsteen sings of how the character is reminded repeatedly throughout the day that a certain aspect of her life is missing - whether it is in activities around the house, through comforting calls from relatives and friends, or during the character's personal quiet time.

...you're missing, when I shut out the lights,

you're missing, when I close my eyes,

you're missing, when I see the sun rise, you're missing...

children are asking if it's all right, will you be in our arms tonight?

To stage this song just by having a character act out the activities

 that Springsteen mentions would be not much more than mimicry. Yet, the song is so strongly evocative of a particular place and time that working in this fashion during some points of the song is almost inescapable. My idea was to embellish and augment the aspects that Springsteen bring to mind, rather than to make my staging subservient to his lyrics.

I did this in two ways. First, I drew from an actor's training method called "The Viewpoints." In this method, which is actually derived

from post-modern dance improvisations of the 1960s but has now developed as an actor's movement training tool and stage blocking device by director Anne Bogart, emotion and relationship of characters onstage is felt to be transmitted not only by the dialogue that they are speaking, but by their physical spacing and distance from each other. The way one person faces or turns away from another, uses body gesture, or is distanced from another - these often unnoticed and implicit relationships speak volumes to us on a sub-conscious level of emotion.

In *You're Missing*, I decided not to compete with the power of Springsteen's story by creating an equally strong movement pattern of my own, but to illustrate the situations he sings about with periodic tableaus. Each pose of the group of dancers (for this song, they could almost be considered as actors rather than dancers), projected the emotion felt by the leading character who was "missing" her lover through the emotion inherent in their physical distance, grouping, and posture. To further embellish this staging device, I creating a general, easy swirling walking pattern between each of the poses that put forth a nebulous feel intermittently throughout the piece. The sharp literal sense of the pose and Springsteen's lyrics were off set by the random walking by the dancers that occurred as a prelude to each newly displayed tableau. The effect was to allow the intensity of Springsteen's situations to emerge spontaneously, as each pose assembled from the random walking on a specific beat of music. Then, upon the break from the pose, the return to random walking gave the viewer a respite from the intense reality, and allowed him to listen more intently to Springsteen's lyrics.

The second way to soften the intense nature of Springsteen's characterization was to create a dual personality for the young, lead character. Rather than having her participate as herself in each tableau, I created another version of the character, but this time older - perhaps by fifteen or twenty years. It was this older character that participated in the tableaus, and the younger version that watched the older version from a short distance away. She was able to see herself and her life in later years - to get a glimpse of her destiny due to the absence of her lover. This younger character moved slowly during the freezes of the tableau, which was valuable in allowing for some continued stage movement during the tableau and preventing a totally static stage scene.

A further manipulation of time occurred during this song occurred when both characters turned to face the memory of the missing person (a specter of the person had appeared within a smoke cloud in the far distance). The younger character had a fresher, more vibrant reaction to the memory, while the older, although still armed with a sharp emotion, was more subdued and resigned to the life of living alone. Their shared emotion of still having hope that at some point their lover would return was highlighted in a slow side-by-side stage walk towards the specter, when the two characters unconsciously took and held hands in a link of their shared desire. At this moment, their similar emotions, although seen years apart, were joined in a present moment exchange.

Although I am inferring that the literal nature of *You're Missing* caused me to create this dual time frame and personality approach, it should be noted that the character motivation, from an acting standpoint, also catalyzed my choice in methods. The thought process behind the feeling of intense emotions is a key element here, and this is something that is hidden in the simplicity of Springsteen's lyrics. Although he may simply state:

Picture's on the night stand, TV's on in the den,

your house is waiting, your house is waiting,

for you to come in...

This description of a home situation speaks volumes in subtext and motivation. It spawned images that allowed me to move in my own choreographic direction. From the phrase "your house is waiting," I instinctively created a living room; compete with children and both younger and older characters, facing the nebulous smoke cloud into which their lover had previously vanished. The assemblage of this tableau, and the forward gripping tension of their bodies, facing the smoke cloud, on the musical point where Springsteen uttered this phrase, created a somber and heart wrenching emotional depiction of the sad state of unfulfilled hope that each character faced. The otherwise perfect family situation was shattered by a "missing" key personality, just waiting to be filled. Springsteen's knack for finding the most direct and simple way to express the exactness of a situation and emotion always results in a powerful emotional response in the listener. His words hit our emotional homes by means of their uncluttered lyric phrasing.

Other Aspects of my Partnership with Springsteen

My creative partnership with Springsteen was also fueled by a great emotionalism in his melodies, rhythms, and orchestrations. This is a vast topic, and it involves a detailed knowledge of musical terminology and theory, one that I am not properly trained to discuss. But I must admit that I instinctively picked up on feelings in Springsteen's backing and instrumental music to create my choreography. For instance, the plaintive cry in the melody of *Empty Sky* urged me to create movement of weariness and despair, while the syncopated percussion cadence of *The Fuse* was the

driving force behind the reptilian, pressured march of the long funeral procession walkers. In the song *Into the Fire*, an ascending four tone pitch on the Springsteen's lyrics "I need your kiss"  (remarkably similar to and perhaps taken from Aaron Copeland's trumpet "call to order" in his *Fanfare for the Common Man*) pushed me to match the character's rising emotional state as he reaches for his lover's face to Springsteen's musical climb. And in *Paradise*, Springsteen's abrupt key change to a faint but high pitched tone, reminiscent of when a hospital heart monitor indicates that the heart beat is no longer present, immediately appealed to me as that moment of both bliss and death – when the suicide bomber explodes his bomb and is instantly killed, yet experiences a fleeting moment of the nirvana he so fervently aspires to. Springsteen again has a knack for composing instrumental and rhythmic patterns that are embedded with great emotion and meaning. Finally, it would be fitting to end by admitting that I also "sampled" many of Springsteen's stage movements for use in my choreography. An examination of my movement for *Mary's Place* will reveal two or three of Springsteen's signature dance moves from his 1984 video of *Dancin' in the Dark*. The movements of the preacher in *Lonesome Day*, *The Rising*, and *Land of Hope and Dreams* clearly uses and builds upon some of Springsteen's proselytizing antics from his performances of *Light of Day*, in particular, and other songs. Perhaps the strongest example comes in *Mary's Place*, when the lead character's joy in finally finding the will to dance again is a direct choreographic reference to Springsteen's upward finger pointing pose, complete with thighs that slap inwardly together, in his exhortation to "turn it up!"

Conclusion

Empty Sky...The Rising is a remarkably complex dance/theatre piece. With it's creative inspiration linked to the music of Bruce Springsteen's *The Rising* and also his song *Land of Hope and Dreams*, and its thematic basis in the events of September 11, 2001, *ESTR* is a performance that can be seen, dismantled, examined, and discussed on many intellectual levels. Although I have given a few examples of how some aspects of the choreography were created, this would amount to a very small portion of the sum of all of the choreography. My work is substantial, but only because the voice that was leading me was substantial. The piece is vast because *The Rising* is a deep, thought provoking, and complex writing. Bruce Springsteen's characters and music resonate with intent, motivation, and immediacy. They cut to the truth and honesty of the situation and of the emotion. They demand that you actively "feel" in order to understand the full extent of his message (Springsteen has often challenged his audience in concerts with the roaring question *"Is anyone alive out there?"*)

Springsteen's compositional choices in writing his lyrics and music have encouraged me to invent new approaches to choreographic creation – both in movement vocabulary and stage composition. He has also, unknowingly, inspired me on a partnership level, to work with him in forming new interpretations of his music and of his thematic ideas. His music, due to its direct honesty, allows me to do so. He doesn't tell the final story – he leaves a great deal of room for my imagination to soar. In that manner, his music is quite generous. Springsteen is both a dreamer and a believer *("my feet, they finally took root in the earth but I got me a nice little place in the stars."* - from his 1973 song *Growin' Up*). And with his music, he manages to make us - his audience - dreamers and believers, too. I know that he has done that with me, as his work filled me with passion for thirty years. His release of *The Rising* inspired me so obsessively that it demanded I stretch the expanses of my abilities to create the 9/11 dance/theatre piece, *Empty Sky...The Rising*, and in doing so, allow me to invent new approaches and methods of dance/theatre choreography.

30
THE FREESTYLE DANCE CLASS
OF EUGENE LORING

by Robert Boross

Dance Chronicle – Vol. 29, Number 2, 2006, Copyright Bob Boross

In today's world, dancers are versatile: ballet dancers work with modern dance choreographers, modern dancers study ballet, and jazz and theatre dancers are required to be proficient in multiple techniques. To be employable, dancers must train in numerous techniques and be capable of instantly absorbing the unique movement characteristics of any choreographer, regardless of form or style of dance. Although top level ballet companies may still sponsor training schools that focus heavily on ballet technique, most dance academies offer well rounded instruction in ballet, modern, jazz, tap, and other forms of dance, and encourage their students to become proficient in many dance areas.

In the United States this willingness to explore movement outside the boundary of a single dance form blossomed in the 1940s and 50s. Spurred by the intersection of classical and modern techniques, and the underlying effects of African-American jazz dance, the metaphor of the "melting pot" of America also applied to the "melting pot" of American dance movement techniques. Pioneering multi-disciplinary American commercial choreographers ignored traditional dictums that corralled students into mastering just one movement technique, and forged personal movement techniques that drew from various dance heritages. Notably, Katherine Dunham created her West Indian and modern dance based technique, as did Jack Cole with his East Indian, modern, and jazz dance inspired technique. Dunham and Cole also relied on African-American rhythm and movement in their amalgamations. In spite of these advances, many traditionalists in the ballet world still carefully guarded the purity of their technique, scorning the study or influence of modern or jazz dance.

*   (In The Shapes of Change: Images of American Dance (Berkeley and Los Angeles: University of California Press, 1979), Marcia Siegel notes the division of technical study with "The 1950s saw the last defense of various stylistic territories to which the first generation of American dancers had staked their claims, a defense that was doomed and therefore all the more tenacious. Till then, ballet, modern, and jazz were separate dance entities that came together with trepidation and co-existed self-consciously at best" (p. 248).*

In a daring move, however, one ballet-based choreographer did see merit in freeing the body from the limitations of mastering just one pedagogic method, and developed a movement technique class that drew from modern, jazz, and other dance influences as well as ballet. Eugene Loring (1911-1982) was an American who first danced with Fokine and Balanchine in the 1930s, and emerged as a choreographer for Lincoln Kirstein's Ballet Caravan and Ballet Theatre before going on to work on Broadway (including Carmen Jones and Silk Stockings) and then in films. In 1947 he founded the American School of Dance in Los Angeles, where he introduced a hybrid, exploratory dance movement technique that he called "freestyle." Loring's freestyle class was a vanguard in exploring the fusion of Euro-centric ballet and modern dance techniques and a forerunner of the new jazz dance techniques of the 1950s. Loring's desire to map out new areas in dance even led him to create his own form of dance notation, which he called "Kinesiography."

(The American School of Dance was one of a new breed of dance training facilities, offering classes in ballet, modern, freestyle, acting, stage makeup, dramatic dance, dance history, choreography, and fledgling jazz dance classes. The school sponsored regular evening showings of dance on film, as well as workshops with noted film and concert choreographers. It was set apart from the typical Hollywood commercial dance studio by its emphasis on concert style dance training.)

Considering his achievements and impact, surprisingly little has been written on Loring and even less on his freestyle class. A two-part article by Olga Maynard in 1966 for *Dance Magazine* discusses the freestyle philosophy, but without describing the actual components of the class.(1) Some articles in the quarterly newsletters of the American School of Dance from 1947-53 add more only to the philosophic description of the class. In them, faculty members Ernest Flatt and Barbara Bailey [Plunk] are highlighted for their personal versions of freestyle, while Marie Bryant (a former Katherine Dunham dancer), Anna Austin (a former Jack Cole dancer), and even Cole himself, while not openly following Loring's freestyle syllabus, were singled out for concurrently teaching their own mélange of jazz, ballet, modern, and ethnic dance forms at Loring's school. Fortunately for this preliminary examination of freestyle, the Eugene Loring papers, held in the Special Collections Library of the University of California, Irvine, have yielded precious information in the form of notes from early staff meetings on the creation of the freestyle technique, as did syllabi from the University of California, Irvine Dance Department, which Loring founded and where freestyle classes were taught from 1965 to the late 1980s. Most of my information, however, has come from interviews with long time Loring associates Barbara Bailey Plunk and James Penrod.(2)

Born in Milwaukee, Wisconsin, Eugene Loring studied acting in his youth with Russian émigré Boris Glagolin and soon moved to New York to study dance. Although he did eventually act on Broadway in William Saroyan's *The Beautiful People* (1941), Loring's career as a dancer began in many important ballets of the 1930s and 1940s: Michel Fokine's *Carnaval*; George Balanchine's *Alma Mater, Reminiscence,* and *The Card Party*; Lew Christensen's *Filling Station*; Adoph Bolm's *Peter and the Wolf*; and Agnes de Mille's *Three Virgins and a Devil*. It rapidly evolved to include choreographing for Ballet Caravan - *Harlequin for President* (1936), *Yankee Clipper* (1937), *Billy The Kid* (1938), and *City Portrait* (1939). He collaborated with Saroyan on *The Great American Goof* (1940) for Ballet Theatre, creating a ballet in which the dancers also were required to deliver lines. His best-known work remains the innovative *Billy the Kid*, with music by Aaron Copland, his homage to the mythic western outlaw. Marcia Siegel heralded Loring's groundbreaking multi-disciplinary approach to movement by describing *Billy the Kid* as "the first great American storytelling ballet . . . [which] invents its own particular form rather than follow the traditional forms of narrative ballet."(3)

Wishing to escape the restrictive policies then current on the mutual study of ballet and modern dance, Loring's bold innovations ignored the defined boundaries between dance forms and other performance genres in *Billy* and *The Great American Goof*. In 1941 he created Dance Players, a visionary company of dancers he trained in ballet, modern, and acting movement techniques. Comprised of prominent dancers like Janet Reed, Joan McCracken, Michael Kidd, Zachary Solov, and Lew Christensen, the company performed dance pieces that melded these various influences - all in service of bringing the unique American spirit to life on stage. Its success, although spectacular, was short-lived, disbanding in November 1942. In 1943 Loring moved to Los Angeles, having been offered a unique six-way contract by MGM as an actor, dancer, choreographer, director, writer, and instructor. In all, he choreographed seventeen films including director Vincente Minnelli's *Yolanda and the Thief* (1945) and *Ziegfeld Follies* (1946), Roy Rowlands's quirky Dr. Seuss fable *The 5000 Fingers of Dr. T.* (1953), Stanley Donen's *Deep in My Heart* (1954), Rouben Mamoulian's *Silk Stockings* (1957), and the ballet choreography for the dances performed by Cyd Charisse in Minelli's *The Band Wagon* (1953)(4). In 1953 he also he created the ballet *Capital of the World*, based on a short story by Ernest Hemingway and with a score by George Antheil, for the prestigious television show *Omnibus* and at the same time staged it for Ballet Theatre.

Influenced by his early acting training with Glagolin and his time in New York dancing in Fokine's ballets, Loring felt the need for a dancer who was not limited in movement possibility by one technique, and who was not hampered by the ornamentation, in particular, of older forms of ballet choreography. Dance movement for the stage and movies at that time was eclectic, and Loring wanted dancers to be able to execute any movement a choreographer might ask for - whether it be from ballet, modern, jazz, or ethnic, or a unique combination - as required by the unique nature of each project. He demanded that the dancer be able to execute what he deemed to be the "truth" of the movement - motivated by feeling and awareness of the how and why the movement was being executed. As paraphrased by journalist Kimmis Hendrick, Loring felt that "dance today...tends to follow no one school. It calls constantly for a merging of classical, modern, and folk techniques. Consequently, it requires of the student tolerance and understanding. It offers most success to the man or woman who seeks to become a "whole person" in the full cultural meaning of the phrase."(5)

In order to bridge the gap between historically separate movement patterns and emerging idiosyncratic personal styles, Loring devised the eclectic technique class that he called freestyle ("one word, no quotes") (6), which was a pillar of Loring's dance training syllabus at the American School of Dance, and subsequently at the University of California, Irvine. This technique was an innovative attempt to integrate the essences of ballet, modern, jazz, and other ethnic forms of dance - a search to discover the common elements among each dance form and develop a shared language between the disparate cultural traditions. In addition, it challenged the dancer to see and create dance movement not from its restrictive pedagogical guidelines but from its limitless possibilities. With freestyle dance, Loring was integrating dance forms, as well as racial and intellectual viewpoints, pre-dating the integration of American social and racial divides that followed in the 1950s and 1960s.

As Loring espoused a very democratic and American ideal that all dance forms were valid and worthy of study and understanding, freestyle was a diverse movement technique, based on a philosophy of social inclusiveness, adherence to truth in application, and treating each dance form with a respect for its unique heritage. The class was purposely nebulous in structure, enabling each teacher of freestyle to add movement elements that were the specialty of the teacher, as well as to tailor the class to the particular needs of the students. For example, Loring's freestyle classes naturally leaned more towards aspects drawn from ballet and acting, while Loring's Graham-trained assistant James

177

Penrod added elements from the Graham technique. In later years former Loring dancer Matt Mattox created his own version of freestyle dance from aspects of the East Indian, modern, and the jazz dance movement of choreographer Jack Cole, along with influences from his own knowledge of ballet and tap dance.

(Although Mattox is generally known as a "jazz" or "modern jazz" dancer, he himself more accurately calls his work "freestyle" dance.)

Freestyle was controversial with many ballet purists, as it was seen as a re-interpretation or a substitute for traditional ballet technique. Loring's intention, however, was not to subvert or supplant ballet technique, but to additionally "train the whole dancer in an entire range of dance techniques." Freestyle was not a substitute for traditional ballet technique (which Loring also taught in separate classes), but a new, multi-disciplinary approach to current choreographic demands. His influence on dance and dancers in Hollywood and stage musicals of the 1940s and 50s, in terms of level of technical ability and sophistication in choreography, was immense. Musicals were set in a wide range of geographic locations and time periods, requiring a wide variety of styles of dance, so that a dancer who succumbed to training in just one form of dance was not valuable to a movie choreographer facing the time constraints of fast paced rehearsals. Freestyle dance was Loring's answer to this - a method that would instill in the dancer basic patterns in movement that were usable in multiple styles of choreography, while creating an adaptive movement response ability. This resulted in the dancers' enhanced versatility in picking up the peculiarities of any requisite movement. Freestyle created well rounded, informed dancers and eliminated the mental prejudice of dancers towards unknown or different dance forms.

Another important aspect of movie choreography then was the creation of movement that reflected both everyday and unusual characters. In Loring's choreography, this could be a group of South American rumba dancers in *Yolanda and the Thief*, a combination of Russian folk steps and jazz syncopation for café dancers in *Silk Stockings*, or the creation of odd movements to illustrate the quirky characters of the children's book author Dr. Seuss in *The 5000 Fingers of Dr. T.* Even as far back as *Billy The Kid,* Loring was creating unique movement on a project by project basis, that melded traditional dance techniques with the dancer's ability to project a character. By combining ideas from acting techniques with theatrical dance movement, Loring was one of a handful of respected dance artists of the time, such as Jerome Robbins, Katherine Dunham, Jack Cole, and Bob Fosse, who were instrumental in establishing the presence of the technically savvy character dancer.

Considering Loring's frequent choreographic forays into American themes and personalities, it is logical that he approached the training of a new breed of American dancer with those same typically American qualities. Loring was a charismatic, inspiring teacher on a mission - to re-shape existing dance training methodologies and movement styles, whether foreign or homegrown, into a single system that would more accurately reflect the idealistically diverse American persona. Students from that time still marvel at how Loring's classes resonated with his heightened energy, enthusiasm, and adventurous spirit. Olga Maynard described Loring as being "…without question so highly regarded that he has come to be an almost legendary figure."(7) Marian Horosko, a student of Loring during her short stint as a Hollywood film dancer, remembers:

> *I found that Gene's class took the professional dancer to another level. There were some fine teachers in LA, but they taught the less professional and were very traditional. When Gene walked into the classroom, usually in a rush, he brought with him energy and enthusiasm to begin to see what we could discover together in the next few minutes. You knew you were there to work, to find new shapes and new approaches to the ballet vocabulary. The breakdown at the barre, beginning with breathing and stretches on the floor, prepared you for an adventure in reshaping, rethinking and reaffirming your dedication to precise, clean, musical interpretation in even the slightest exercise. Loring himself demonstrated and crossed his studio in two steps with his freedom of movement, his openness, and joy in moving. He smiled and you smiled. He was the choreographer-pedagogue, more than a teacher. Loring was the East Coast's loss and he should have had more opportunity and support here [NY]. It was typical of him to bring film dance to*

a new level when he worked in LA. Everyone fell under his spell and superlative requirements. He wanted your utmost concentration and commitment, even in class work, and you gave it to him.(8)

The Freestyle Class

The American School of Dance received its license to open for business on October 15, 1947,(9) and the first advertisement for the freestyle class was in the Hollywood Citizen newspaper, mentioning that a "Free tech." class was to begin on Tuesday, July 6, 1948, from 11:30-1 pm.(10) Although this may be the initial occurrence of a commercially available freestyle class, aspects of Loring's freestyle instruction were offered earlier, in a less codified form, from 1941-43 in training the Dance Players dancers,* and possibly even as early as 1938 in preparing his dancers for the unusual angular movement in his groundbreaking *Billy The Kid*.(11)

*(In "Eugene Loring's Very American School of Dance,"(Dance Magazine, August 1956, p.33) Margaret Lloyd and Selma Jeanne Cohen state that during Loring's Dance Players company retreat in the woods of Pennsylvania in 1941, the company "utilized free style [sic] technique, drawing on the full movement range of the human body. The Loring style draws no line between ballet and modern dance.")

Early versions of the class can be reconstructed from the remembrances of Barbara Bailey Plunk, a ballet teacher and dancer for stage, film, and early television. A longtime Loring assistant, she began teaching the class at the American School of Dance in 1950. In addition, held in the Eugene Loring Collection at the University of California, Irvine are notes from five faculty meetings on the freestyle syllabus, chronologically beginning with "4th meeting - Nov. 27" and culminating on January 21. No years are given, but given the exploratory tone of the discussion notes, I would speculate that they come from the formative 1947-48 period. A later version of the class, as taught at UC Irvine in the 1970s and 80s, can be found in a codified syllabus that lists exercise concepts for classes in two levels.

Since the class was exploratory, and a basic premise was to allow each teacher to contribute aspects from their particular strengths and interests, the syllabus consisted of concepts, actions, general movements, and patterns rather than actual exercises set to counts. Each teacher had the freedom to create unique exercises based on the general characteristics, although according to Plunk, most teachers drew from Loring's example as a basic template. Loring also would watch all teachers in order to approve their version of the freestyle class.

The initial syllabus discussions covered a range of ideas, one of which was to examine and either use or discard concepts and movements from other established techniques. For instance, in the fourth meeting of Nov. 27, references are made to positive aspects of the Lester Horton technique (as in adding vocal, animal sounds to movement that are consistent with the quality of the movement) and well as negative (it was felt that Horton's use of the word "curl" for spreading of the toes was "illogical"). Cecchetti's eight basic movements of "lower, rise, bend, stretch, jump, turn, glide, and dart" are mentioned. There is also a list of twenty-two movement concepts as defined by Emile Jaques-Dalcroze. From the January 14th meeting, a discussion on accurate terminology for the various executions of a contraction within the body includes the statement that while a Graham "contraction" was permitted in the class, it would be more accurately defined as a "directed tension."

The overwhelming gist of the discussions, however, was to examine, in a scientific fashion, how many ways that the body could move - whether in adaptations of existing dance techniques or in new movement. The use of isolation of body parts was suggested as a prime exploratory device, and it was expressed that further investigation involving isolation would expand on their initial findings. Also, an idea consistent with Loring's choreographic vision of creating dances with American themes and characters was to perform balletic movements and positions in a parallel alignment - without the use of outward rotation in the hip and shoulder sockets - and to rename these parallel movements with English language terminology. Therefore, a tendu, when executed in a parallel position, became a "foot brush." Similarly, a retiré became a "hinge" and a développé became a "leg unfolding," while an enveloppé became a "leg folding." The ballet attitude became a "triangle," as did as the floor position more commonly known in early modern dance as a swastika. To plié in the parallel position was referred to as "to descend."

Plunk remembered that freestyle classes in the 1950s were accompanied by drum rhythms, often played by the instructor. They began with center floor warm ups that utilized specific breathing, inhaling and exhaling while the body rolled up from a rounded over position to an erect standing position and back down again. This could be combined with movements to open and close the chest, and also contractions (directed tensions) with open and closed elbows, while in the erect position. Floor exercises were also introduced at this point in the class. The hips were loosened with stretches in the lotus position. Spinal articulation was enhanced with a floor exercise that began with the dancer lying supine, rolling up through the vertebra to bring the torso to a lengthened sitting position, and then rolling back down through the vertebrae to the initial flat position. Additional spinal work on the floor included having the dancer lay on the side of the body and stretching from a fetal position to a fully arched position. Leg and hip joints were further warmed on the floor with folding and unfolding movements performed in parallel alignment, or developpé and enveloppé in turned out alignment. Sit-ups, which according to Plunk were uncommon in dance classes for that time period, were also given.

From there the dancer would move to the barre, and begin exercises that included flat backs and rolling actions of the spine, side stretches away from the barre, and Achilles' tendon stretches. Descents, the parallel version of pliés, were executed in the standard positions of first, second, third, fourth open, fourth closed, and fifth. Level I was for beginners, who would only execute a half descent and lift, in both the parallel and turned out alignment in order to understand the difference in feeling. The barre work would then proceed to parallel foot stretches (like tendus) in front, side, and back directions, as well as parallel leg stretches (like dégagés) and leg circles (like rond de jambes). Hinges were next, and a half hinge was similar to a parallel coupé and a full hinge was a parallel retiré. Accents in execution, putting the emphasis on the opening or the closing of the movement, were covered. The barre concluded with leg swings, which could be either grand rond de jambes or balançoires executed in a parallel alignment.

The dancer then returned to the center of the room to begin isolated body movements - head, shoulders, rib cage, and pelvis. (Plunk remarked on the attitude of the class to the hip movements by saying "In 1950, moving your hips front and back was a little rude. Elvis hadn't hit the scene yet, so we were always embarrassed about that.") But the isolations were performed in a clinical fashion, without any sexual connotations.

The class continued in the center floor with a repeat of many of the barre exercises for the beginner level. Loring also would encourage the understanding of the division of movement according to the planes of the body, with his "Division of Body Circles." In this, he would imagine the standing body to be at the center of a clock, with 12 o'clock directly in front of the body, and 6 o'clock directly behind. Using this image, Loring would direct movement to different "hours" of the clock. Plunk used this analogy to comment on how Loring desired to increase the range of the body, for example with leg circles on the floor passing from 11 o'clock to 7 o'clock, rather than the typical ballet pedagogic method of performing rond de jambes in half circles, from 12 to 6 o'clock.

More advanced freestyle dancers encountered more challenging movement in the center portion. Dancers were encouraged to think and improvise on finding new ways to perform or execute movements. New ways of descending or emerging from the floor, for instance, or new ways to turn - perhaps in the horizontal plane rather than in a vertical plane. Isolation played a prominent role in expanding the movement possibilities of body parts. Dancers within the class would offer suggestions or incorporate the inventions of fellow classmates. Loring drew from his training as an actor to give improvisations reminiscent of his early theatre work with Glagolin by having dancers imitate each other in mirrored movement. Another exercise would be to stand back to back with an unknown dancer, then to turn quickly, and react spontaneously to the shock of the new face. In this way, emotional reactions were tied to physical movements, and a verbal discussion on the veracity of the reaction would ensue. In a similar vein, dancers often were given homework assignments, in which they would observe people in everyday jobs, memorize their movements, and perform those movements in class while fellow dancers tried to guess the profession from the movements. Attention was always given to careful observance of line and design and shapes in space.

This extended center portion of class was a laboratory research time for teachers and students. Depending on the teacher and the needs of the class, this portion might focus on the improvisations and acting exercises, as well as work on cataloging dramatic qualities or movements involving opposing rhythms. Or, a teacher might give a more elaborate final combination of movements taken from the class exercises as well as movement created by dancers in the class. Plunk said that she used this time in her beginner classes to try out her choreography for professional singers. The class concluded with a cool down consisting of a return to the initial breathing exercises, coupled with the body rolling up and down. Exams were given once a year to determine if the dancer was prepared to move to the next level.

In terms of movement instruction, Loring was adamant that the movement aspects and ornamentation that define a particular choreographer's style, or form of dance, or time period of invention were to be stripped from the body in freestyle dance. Plunk felt that "Eugene was very independent in that he wanted his style based on necessity, based on clean lines, even in ballet – no artificiality, you just teach the basic, you teach plain movement so that you can dress it. The body is a dress mold that you put the character on. And that was his whole philosophy."

The later incarnation of Loring's freestyle class at the University of California, Irvine, was described by another Loring associate, James

Penrod. Beginning in 1955 Penrod had worked closely with Loring, teaching freestyle at the American School of Dance and later in defining the curriculum at UC Irvine. Along with ballet, Loring included freestyle as a core technique - in place of modern dance techniques. (Modern dance was not entirely absent, though. Penrod's freestyle classes, due to his strong proficiency in Graham modern dance technique, naturally leaned to principles from Graham's method.)

The syllabi for the UC Irvine classes of the 1970s and 80s reveal concepts to be covered in a freestyle class, without reference to specific exercise patterns or class order. Most of the class is consistent with concepts found in other dance techniques. The level I class consisted of "full pliés, leg circles on floor [parallel rond de jambe à terre], leg circle off floor [parallel rond de jambe en l'air], leg unfolding, leg folding, accents [musical execution], leg rotations, isolation [ribs, head, hips, shoulders], sway, contraction (note that here the movement was not called a "directed tension"), impulse [rebound, action/reaction], ripple action, division of body circles, torso circles, body design, moving designs, qualities [dynamics], forces, pivot turns [paddle or pencil turns], rhythmic patterns [in movement or with clapping], kneeling positions, standing to kneeling, knee and sitting transition, off balance fall, falls, jumping, prone roll, improvisation, sitting positions, and "other work" - which may include special exercises by the instructor, as well as a cool down and breathing."

Level II freestyle classes were to include stretches, coordinations, quick footwork, space patterns, division of body circles, leg extensions on half toe, swings, rhythms, oblique pliés, "T" positions, off balance positions, spirals, falls, descending splits, coccyx balance turns, hip pivots, progression of knee turns, squatting, rolling, qualities, improvisation, combinations, jumps, leg hinges with big circles, level awareness, torso articulation, and other work.

The syllabi from the UC Irvine freestyle classes embody the same basic concepts as the earlier versions of the class, although over time at UC Irvine the class slowly shifted to a lessened emphasis on acting and non-dance influences and more emphasis on structured dance technique. Penrod became the chair of the department upon Loring's resignation in 1979, but with Loring's diminishing influence at UCI and increasing pressure to instill mainstream modern dance classes, Penrod felt that the term freestyle became too difficult to define to students unaware of its history. Freestyle was softened to "freestyle modern dance" and eventually dropped from the curriculum in the late 1980s, to be replaced by more popular modern dance and jazz dance techniques.

LEGACY OF FREESTYLE

An important aspect of the freestyle technique was the addition of new movement vocabulary to the choreographer's palette by exploring movement in the parallel alignment of the hip socket. Venturing away from the turned-out alignment of ballet, Loring investigated movements performed in the alignment more typical of normal human locomotion and characterization. When compared to movements from the better known modern dance styles of the period (Graham, Humphrey, Limón), Loring's freestyle held less identifiable stylistic flair. The movement technique in the first portion of his class reflected the anatomic movements of the body, without ornamentation or emotion. Class time spent on exploration of the emotive aspects of the body followed this initial basic work. Plunk's comment on how Loring desired the body to be trained as a "dress mold" - with no ornamentation or added style, and was therefore ready to be adorned with the style pertinent to each choreographic project - reveals the goal of Loring's movement training, and of the nature of the class movement exercises. Unlike ballet or modern dance of that era, freestyle looked ahead to post-modern philosophies that allowed for the inclusion of any body movement in dance choreography.

Like Lester Horton, another Los Angeles choreographer/teacher, Loring enjoyed his relative obscurity on the

West Coast and did not seek to publicize his work widely in New York. Although freestyle's effect in its own incarnation was not long lasting or geographically widespread, the openness of the class to experimentation and creativity did have a significant effect on the future work of its teachers and students. Many became respected choreographers, or moved on to develop new, more codified training methods of their own, with the freestyle philosophy reflected in their work. To name just a few, choreographers and teachers who have been closely influenced by freestyle include Matt Mattox, Ernest Flatt, Jack Tygett, Paul Gleason, Marie Bryant, Don Bradburn, Jolene Wendell, Roy Fitzell, and Israel "El" Gabriel, as well as Penrod and Plunk. Eugene Facciuto, better known as "Luigi" - the creator of a prominent jazz dance technique - credits Loring as exposing him to the "Fokine ballet approach."(12) Luigi danced in Loring's film *The Toast of the Town* in 1950, and Plunk remembered that Luigi was a student at the American School of Dance during the early 1950s and most likely would have been aware of the class (13). In another application of the freestyle philosophy, the director/dancer Joanne Tewksbury also taught a freestyle dance class that favored movement for actors. George Chakiris, a versatile film dancer who played Bernardo 1961 film *West Side Story*, was a scholarship student at the school and therefore would have included freestyle classes in his training regimen. Another person influenced by Loring was dance historian Selma Jeanne Cohen, a long time Loring associate who studied freestyle dance and frequently gave lectures on dance history at the school.

The spirit of openness to new movement ideas championed by freestyle dance was a catalyst for the formation of new movement ideas that emerged in the 1950s, one being the burgeoning field of what was called "modern jazz dance." Here, elements from jazz music and vernacular jazz dance movement vocabulary merged with ideas from ballet and modern for use on the commercial and concert stage. Depending on the approach of each individual modern jazz dance creator, the philosophy of freestyle, or mixing the valid and truthful elements of many movement forms to create an individual, expressive invention, was in effect at the core of modern jazz dance.

187

The legacy of freestyle dance remains rooted in its insistence on breaking away from old traditions of dance movement that did not suit a new American posture and physicality. Loring was adamant in his desire to create a unique synthesis of dance forms that would reflect the composite American population. Like America, it required a blend of the core of ideas from many sources that would coalesce as a new unified vision of valid, motivated movement. It reflected the American ideas of diversity and respect for all heritages, and held the basic assumption that all movement forms, regardless of origin, had elements that were welcomed in the formation of a new way of dance training and expression.

NOTES

1. Olga Maynard, "Eugene Loring Talks to Olga Maynard". *Dance Magazine*, July 1966, pp. 35-39 and "Eugene Loring Talks to Olga Maynard —Part II. *Dance Magazine*, August 1966, pp. 52-54, 72-74.

2. Barbara Bailey Plunk, Personal Interview. September 8, 2004; James Penrod, Personal Interview. September 20, 2004.

3. Marcia B. Siegel. *The Shapes of Change: Images of American Dance.* University of California Press. Berkeley and Los Angeles, California. 1979. p.118.

4. In a letter to the author, undated but probably 1995, Matt Mattox said "even if Michael Kidd did most of the choreography for 'Band Wagon,' it was Eugene Loring who did the ballet sequence when I danced with Cyd Charisse."

5. Kimmis Hendrick, *Theater and Dance – Famed Choreographer Poses Test Question.* n.d. Eugene Loring Special Collection, University of California, Irvine Library, Irvine, CA.

6. Quoted in: Marian Horosko, "Loring The Teacher," *Dance Magazine*, November 1988, p. 46.

7. Olga Maynard, "Eugene Loring Talks to Olga Maynard". *Dance Magazine*, July 1966, p. 35.

8. Horosko, Marian. Personal correspondence. January 23, 2006.

9. "Three Years Old." *American School of Dance News*, Vol.1, No. 2. November 1950. Eugene Loring Special Collection, University of California, Irvine Library, Irvine, CA.

10. Box 210S, Eugene Loring Special Collection, University of California, Irvine Library, Irvine, CA.

11. Barbara Bailey Plunk, Personal Interview.

12. Luigi; Kreigel, Lorraine Person; Roach, Francis James. *Luigi's Jazz Dance Warm Up and Introduction to Jazz Dance Style and Technique*. Princeton Book Publishers. Pennington, NJ. 1997. p. xv.

13. Luigi's jazz dance technique shows ballet and modern dance influences, as does Mattox's version of freestyle technique. Alvin Ailey was exposed to Loring's philosophies when he danced in Loring's uncredited choreography for the film version of *Carmen Jones* (1954). Jerome Robbins, who had worked with Loring in the first years of Ballet Theatre and had danced the role of Alias in *Billy the Kid*, followed a parallel track, with his training in Russian ballet and acting methods. The movement inventions for his ballet *Fancy Free* and his many Broadway shows demonstrate a philosophical basis consistent with Loring's. Other prominent dancers creating modern dance styles that reflected the freestyle philosophy include Gus Giordano, Talley Beatty, Donald McKayle, Bob Fosse, and Peter Gennaro.

31
SUE SAMUELS AND JO JO SMITH
THE BEGINNINGS OF THE SMITH/SAMUELS TECHNIQUE AND BROADWAY DANCE CENTER

by Bob Boross

Jazz Dance E-News – September 2008, Copyright Bob Boross

Find a long-time jazz teacher, scratch the surface, and you'll most

likely find a treasure of valid historical information on the development of jazz dance. That's what I recently did as I made a connection with Sue Samuels, who has been a fixture teaching jazz dance at Broadway Dance Center, the Ailey School, and Manhattan Motion Dance Studios in NYC for more than thirty years. But her roots in NYC jazz go even deeper, as her exposure to jazz dance dates back to the dawn of the 1970s and her association with the noted teacher Jo Jo Smith. Smith was a powerful jazz/Latin dancer who mixed jazz with martial arts movements. He choreographed for stage and film, including *Saturday Night Fever* with John Travolta. He also is significant for founding his own studio in the 1960s – Jo Jo's Dance Factory. This studio morphed through various incarnations and eventually became the legendary

Broadway Dance Center. My inquiry into the Smith-Samuels technique uncovered a long lost interview of the two from 1970 where Smith explains and demonstrates his martial arts approach, and Smith shows a Latin inspired phrase. I was able to persuade Samuels to post the video on *YouTube* for general viewing and a link to that video is provided at the end of this interview, along with links to Samuels personal website, and ways to order DVDs of her classwork.

But for now, here is the story of the technique of Jo Jo Smith and Sue Samuels, and the history of Broadway Dance Center.

1- Sue, what year did you come to NYC and who were the teachers you were studying with?

I came to New York in 1968 to follow my dream of performing on Broadway. The teachers I studied with at that time were: Ballet with Madame Swoboda, at the Ballet Russe de Monte Carlo, and Jazz with Jo Jo Smith.

2 - How did you come to meet Jo Jo Smith, and how did you begin to work together on Jo Jo's Dance Factory?

I was working in many shows with George Reich, traveling around the world. I only had Ballet and Tap training at the time. My friend told me that Jazz training would be good for me and he recommended Jo Jo's classes. I began to attend classes regularly. Even though the jazz style was very different from my ballet training, I loved how the style was "clean." The positions were strong and required my ballet technique to execute the jazz movements. I'm a little embarrassed to say that Jo Jo had an eye for me, and that I became infatuated with his "charm." I fell in love with him. I was committed to him and his style of jazz. After a year or so, I began to teach his beginner level classes. I had prior teaching experience from my ballet company days in Florida. I became the "lead" dancer for Jo Jo's dance company and I also made all of the costumes for the company. I became an assistant to Jo Jo for the company repertory. I had good ideas for staging and he would come up with the steps; we were a team. We also have two children together. My daughter,

Elka Samuels Smith, has a management company for performing artists called Divine Rhythm Productions. My son, Jason Samuels Smith, is an Emmy Award winning tap dancer and choreographer. I also have a wonderful dancing granddaughter, Kaia, who is 5 years old.

We found a place to rent on the west side on 50th street between 11th-12th avenues. It was an old factory building that inspired the name for Jo Jo's Dance Factory. There was no heat in the winter and I remember having to put up plastic over the windows in the winter to keep the studios warm. The "diehard's" came. Back in those days, the area was not much more than factories and a couple of diners. After the company was hired to perform with Johnny Halliday in Paris, we were able to invest in a bigger place on Broadway and 55th street. After one year of being there, we received a notice from the landlord that they would be demolishing the building. We went looking for a new place close by and there was a landlord right on the next block at 1733 Broadway who felt intrigued about having a dance studio in his building. He was really helpful in the transition because we no longer had the same funds to invest the way we had at the other place. We did all the work ourselves laying down the floors. We worked really hard to get one studio up and running just to help generate income. Slowly we were able to build up to 4 studios, with a reception area, changing rooms w/showers, and an organic health food juice bar that was run by my sister Judy called Josue's juice bar. We wanted to expose the dancers to healthy food options right on the premises. The smell of whatever my sister was cooking on location would pass through the rooms while we were dancing and as soon as the classes were finished the dancers would run over to the juice bar to see what it was. At some point the movie *The Fan* with Lauren Bacall was shot at the studio. Also, we rehearsed for *Saturday Night Fever* and most of the dancers that were in the film were all from the studio. Slowly, the dance business started changing. At this time all the teachers had their own studios but the real estate begin to rise and the teachers couldn't afford to maintain their own places any longer. I was walking in the street and saw Frank Hatchett walking toward me with a gloomy look on his face. He told me that the studio he and Henry LeTang had been renting was no longer available and he had no place to teach his large group of students for his next class. I said that I had an idea, just wait right here. I went upstairs where Jo Jo was and I convinced Jo Jo to let Frank rent space from us. That was unheard of in that time for teachers to share the same space, especially competing jazz styles. With some hesitation, Jo Jo agreed to let Frank come and teach his classes at our studio. That was just the beginning of a new era in dance studios in New York. After that, Trutti Gasparinetti, came to teach ballet, Judy Bassing came to teach tap, Serena taught belly dance, and there were several other teachers who also came to rent space. This started to create an environment where dancers could come for all their dance needs under one roof. What developed was almost unintentional, but it sparked a trend in the way major New

York City dance studios are today. With all of the growing business, it became bigger than what Jo Jo and I felt we could handle and Frank offered to take over with the Hines brothers (Gregory and Maurice) as partners, called the Hatchett-Hines Performing Arts Center. The same thing happened to them where the business needs were just to great to be able to handle and maintain careers as artists, but little did we know, that an older man that was taking our beginner level classes named Richard Ellner would be the man for the job. He was a business man who loved to take class and he was able to take over for Frank and grow the business while maintaining the integrity and joy of dance. The studio was really named "The Rhythm of Life" which was based off of one of the numbers in the Broadway Musical *Sweet Charity*, but it became known worldwide as Broadway Dance Center.

3 - Please try to describe the technique you both developed, in its earliest version, and how it evolved to what you are teaching today?

Jo Jo had an existing jazz style when I met him. Jo Jo lacked in "classical" training and got a lot of his "lines" from his Karate training. When I became so involved, he saw his work done with a "classical" flair. His "jazz barre" was rough because of the order and execution of movements which did not allow enough warm-up for the muscles. Jo Jo appreciated my classical training and listened to my suggestions of changing the order of many of the barre exercises as well as transitions into the movements for a better flow overall. Also, the way I performed the movements inspired him to do choreography specifically for women.

4 - What are the particular "jazz" qualities that you try to bring out in your work?

The qualities that I emphasize in my work include clean, controlled lines that help to create strong visual statements. One of the most important elements is "musicality," where the movements allow the dancer to actually "sing the music with their body" while doing the choreography. I believe that jazz dance originally consisted of many facets including Latin, Lyrical, Funky, Swing, Theatre and Classical jazz moves and I like to include them all in my classes and my body of work.

5 - What are the reasons for your long-term success in NYC as a jazz dance teacher?

I feel that I have lasted so long in NYC because I take my time in class to actually teach the student as an individual. I am not just dancing in front of them. I explain to them the energy of the movements and how to find the flow. I also take time to make sure they are clean from one movement to the next without becoming "stiff." I teach the "mind-body" connection and the different techniques of "picking up" the choreography. My classes attract a diverse body of students. Many of my students train for Broadway and professional careers, but there are also several students who dance for fun and/or health benefits.

6 - What obstacles do you feel have hindered jazz dance in its development?

What factors are helping to push it forward in its evolution?

I'm not really sure that there are any obstacles hindering the development of jazz dance. Dance in general has been undergoing change for some time now. There are more jazz teachers than ever before. With the different jazz teacher comes a different style. Jazz has changed in so many ways. In the past, jazz dance styles were recognizable. You were able to identify the work just from watching the choreography. These days, jazz styles are very similar to each other, many being "lyrical" in nature. In the past, we did many genres of movements in the class. Latin, funky, lyrical, and theatrical besides jazzy. Most upcoming teachers don't offer different genres within the same class. If you want Latin, you must attend a Latin class. If you want theater, you must attend a theater class and so on. I think that all of the dance shows on television is helping to expose more about the field, and making more people want to dance just for the fun of it.

7 - Are you optimistic or pessimistic about the future evolution of jazz dance?

I am optimistic! Dance is alive and evolving. I am excited to see all the new aspects being included in dance these days.

8 - What are your plans for your continued work in jazz dance - any new projects or directions?

I plan to continue to teach at Broadway Dance Center, Alvin Ailey and Manhattan Movement and Arts Center. I feel that training the student either for a performing career, or just for the fun and exercise is important, plus, I still love to dance myself! I also want to create more of a performing venue for the "casual" student by creating student showcase choreography opportunities. I would also like to begin rehearsals for the professional dancer by creating a dance company. I have a large repertory which is entertaining and exciting. I have written a musical play for Broadway together with my partner Jorge Barreiro. We have a wonderful script, and GREAT music. The show is for tap and hip hop styles of dance. Bringing together these two styles of dance for Broadway should be something different and very NOW.

9 - Where can people order your technique video and music?

My Jazz Dance Warm-up includes barre exercises, floor exercises, and isolations for an "at home" class experience. Also, it is for the teacher looking for a warm-up which include s technique. The DVD can be ordered online at: www.divinerhythmproductions.com, or by sending me an e-mail to susamjaz@aol.com.

32
JAMES CARLÈS AND HIS
JAZZ NEW CONCEPT

by Bob Boross

Jazz Dance E-News – October 2008, Copyright Bob Boross

Forms of art must move forward, change, and adapt - constantly being re-invented. What is good is kept - what is new is tested, evaluated, and if it has merit, it is welcomed to the body of art in that field. With this in mind, I am pleased to discuss the work of a new rising star in the field of jazz dance- one with a seemingly radical methodology - the dancer and choreographer James Carlès.

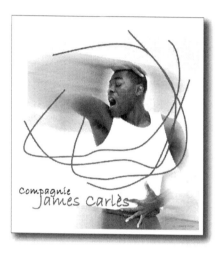

Born in Africa and now settled in Toulouse, France, James Carlès is poised to contribute a unique and most welcome voice to the future of jazz dance. His approach is startlingly fresh - not by way of re-formulating established jazz patterns and launching into unseen territory, but by returning to the roots of jazz dance and re-thinking its choreographic possibilities with a mind trained in a cosmopolitan artistic sensibility. I had the opportunity to observe his work when we were both faculty members of the 3rd International Jazz Dance Forum in Paris, France (2004), and mostly recently again in Paris in 2007 when I asked him about his jazz dance philosophy, which he calls "jazz new concept."

Carlès himself moves like a swirling wind, animated with the invisible molecular dynamics of breath that is blown from his religious gods into the living body of man. His execution shows no effort - completely relaxed and completely free. In this manner his appearance mirrors the forces of the unseen that act on us all, giving physical shape to its imperceptible natural beauty.

Carlès's first exposure to dance was in learning traditional African dances, where every dance has a meaning and a name. As he explained, every African dance has a reason and an identity. But then Carlès felt the need to explore dance and choreography, so he began to study modern and jazz dance. When he asked his jazz dance teacher "What is jazz dance?" the teacher could not come up with a definition as to what it was and what was its meaning. This lack of singular identification in jazz dance philosophy led Carlès to shift his training more to modern dance. He studied in New York at the Limòn Institute and the Alvin Ailey Dance Center, and also in England at the London Contemporary Dance School.

Jazz music was still an inspiration to him, though, and he began to develop his choreographic eye with his personal tools - African and modern dance movement vocabulary, cutting edge choreographic approaches involving minimalism and technology, and the inspiration to move coming from jazz music, particularly John Coltrane. In these lay the building blocks of his "jazz new concept" - mixing the historical African and  Afro-American root movement with a contemporary creative mind, reacting to jazz musical rhythms. Carlès has not really ever studied the traditional jazz dance vocabulary of the American masters - Cole, Mattox, Luigi, etc - so he is in effect creating a form of movement that is identifies with the jazz dance heritage without being part of the status quo of other jazz dance styles.

Carlès founded the James Carlès Centre in Toulouse, France in 1998. His work has been well-received, with funding from the French Ministry of Culture and Communication, the Committee for Cultural Affairs in Midi-Pyrennes, and the General Council of Haute-Garonne. Since this debut, Carlès has founded the Companie James Carlès and directs the International Festival Danse a Toulouse. His research into the early choreographies of Afro-American dance has led to a three year project, *Black Dance(s) & Continent(s)*. During the period 2008-2011 Carlès is directing a project that is recreating and restaging formative dances by Asadata Dafora, Katherine Dunham, Pearl Primus, Talley Beatty, Eleo Pomare, and African star of the early Parisian music hall - Feral Benga.

I would like to close this introduction of the work of James Carlès with his final and possibly most important stated tenet - "Acquired experience is wasted unless it is passed on." This thought is something that all of us as jazz dancers are wrestling with in the face of the debate over new school vs. old school, contemporary vs. classic. Our society is a disposable one, tossing out ideas and products only a decade old in favor of what is new. As we do this over and over, we slowly distance ourselves from the foundation of our existence. A foundation that resonate with unadulterated power and significance. By doing so, we risk losing connection to things that are real and meaningful, in a long lasting fashion. James Carlès recognizes this, and has found a way to assimilate the best of both worlds. With his marriage of African and modern dance movement dynamics and vocabulary, composed with a contemporary cosmopolitan process, and inspired by jazz rhythms – he has found a "jazz new concept" that honors the past while it points towards the future.

33
MICHAEL OWENS
THE BEST KEPT SECRET IN THEATRE JAZZ DANCE

by Bob Boross

Jazz Dance E-News – October 2008, Copyright Bob Boross

Jazz dance at times focuses on what's new and trendy, elevating teachers who can capture the current moment, but who may not have the substance to translate their new recognition into a long, productive career as a teacher that significantly affects the field. Teachers who stand the test of time are ones who back their topical styles with solid dance technique and a longstanding dedication to their art. We've all heard a great deal about the legends in the field - Mattox, Luigi, Giordano, Simonson - and to that stellar roster I'd like to add the name of another fine teacher who has made a tremendous contribution to jazz dance education - the bi-coastal master of a sensual jazz dance style, Michael Owens.

His may not be a household name to those whose dance experience is relegated to dance competitions, but if you were to ask the top jazz dancers on Broadway and in films over the last three decades with whom they studied, the name Michael Owens would surely figure prominently. Owens is a unique figure - his career dates back to 1975 in New York. He spent nearly five years developing his style while teaching in Helsinki, Finland, and Paris, France, and then moving back to NYC in 1981 where he was a mainstay in the Broadway jazz scene with his classes at Douglas Wassell's School of Theatre and Dance and then as director of Jazz Dance at the David Howard Dance Center. In 1997 Owens moved to Los Angeles, where he now teaches daily for Hama's Dance Center in Studio City, the Performing Arts Center in Van Nuys, and at Santa Monica College.

I studied regularly in California with Owens at Hama's Dance Center, and I came to admire his sensual jazz technique and his rapid-fire class combinations. And I should also note his signature razor sharp sense of humor - where any foible of an unsuspecting class taker might be announced to the entire class in an Owens quip that could be embarrassingly risqué, but always delivered with a loving tease to the student.

Originally from Boston, Owens first aspired to be an actor at the Boston Conservatory of Music, but realized that to be employable, he had to do it all - act, sing, and dance. He studied ballet with Dance Dept Chair Ruth Ambrose, and soon found that dance interested him more than acting. Owens made his way to NYC in 1975, studying on scholarship with the Joffrey Ballet, and then with Wilson Morelli at the Morelli Dance School. There he came in to contact with Lynn Simonson, a teacher who was known internationally in jazz circles for her anatomically sound approach to dance training, and her work in improvisation and choreographing to jazz music. Owens credits Simonson as his biggest influence as a teacher. Although their approaches are different, Owens said Lynn taught him "how to correctly construct a class using a thorough warm-up to avoid injury, to create dance combinations that require thought and, most importantly, to care for and respect my students." When asked for her impression of working with Owens, Simonson offered her thoughts with -

Michael Owens is the first person I trained to teach with me in NYC in the early 70's. From the beginning, he was a natural teacher. Then, and now, Michael is a passionate, knowledgeable jazz teacher who always gives 110 %. He cares about his students deeply, and always pushes them to do more, to try more. His style is musical, precise and exact, and he challenges the student to articulate movement with absolute clarity and control. He pretends to be a demanding grouch, but everyone who takes his class feels the love and joy for dance that he shares when he teaches. If

I were only a few years younger, I would be in his class. (Lynn Simonson)

Owens taught at Morelli's with Simonson, and then through her patronage was offered teaching jobs in Helsinki in 1977, and then in Paris. There, Owens observed classes taught by Matt Mattox, modern teacher Peter Goss, and the British jazz teacher Molly Molloy.

With the help of American jazz teachers, jazz dance in Finland was just starting to flourish and Michael Owens was at the forefront. Tarja Rinne, a highly respected Finnish jazz teacher for many decades, was enamored with the young Owens and when I asked about his impact on the Finnish jazz dance scene, she replied:

> *I think the energy, good sense of humor and absolute sense of style have made him success in his career all these years. I met him the last time here in Finland on the 5th Jazz Dance Symposium in Seinäjoki (2006), and I have to say his charm has only grown. Plus the Bob Fosse style he has ambitiously been developing showed really that he is one of real masters in jazz dance today. His influence in jazz dance in Finland has been really something...*

Armed with his newly developing singular teaching method, Owens returned to NYC in 1981 to establish his name as one of the premier jazz dance teachers of the next two decades.

The Michael Owens jazz class, in its current format, starts with a set warm up that works all aspects of the body in both the linear aspect of ballet with the isolation aspect of jazz. The opening movement portion is broken into three sections involving rolling up and down, lateral stretches, contractions, flat backs, and some simple isolations that evoke the classic positions of theatre dance. This portion (about 12 minutes long) is accompanied by a percussive music score composed specifically for his exercises - a score that has been repetitively ingrained in his students so deeply that merely hearing the opening drum beat will cause any Owens student to instinctively launch into the first arm stretches!

The second portion is a tricky combination of footwork, *tendus*, *degages, passé relevés*, and upper body stretches to the front, side, and back. It finishes in a held balance on one foot, always in a new position for each class. The third portion features extended work on isolations - head, shoulders, ribs, hips - and the inclusion of arm coordination with the head isolations. Often adding *tendus* to the head and arm movements, this exercise will challenge the ability of even the most astute dancer.

Owens then takes his dancers to the floor, for more stretches for the spine in floor roll ups, contractions, and twist stretching. He works the abdominals in an extended crunch section, and then has the dancer flip to stomach on the floor for upper body strengthening work that is drawn from yoga - "down dog," "plank," "warrior," etc. But the delivery is surely not relaxing, as Owens reveals his old school roots by accompanying the entire floor section with a hand drum and mallet, pounding out rhythms at ear splitting volume and barking his instructions. This is the point in class where any dancer not living up to his expectations should fear, as any drooping buttock or flabby stomach will become the source of his next sharp skewering.

After a well-deserved water break, the next section of Owens' class is unique to him. Owens teaches a jazz adagio, always featuring leg extensions in *devant, a la seconde*, and *arabesque* positions, and mixed with a slinky jazz style and linear sense. I have found that the control needed to execute fluid but sustained lyrical jazz choreography is often overlooked in so many jazz classes, but here Owens works regularly to increase the ability of his students with this adagio. Always finishing with a held balance on one foot, this portion of the Owens class is on its on worth the price of admission.

Finally its time for the class combination, and here Owens is again singular in his approach. Although no jazz teacher can be completely encapsulated in one description, I think that in his movement style, Owens has found a unique niche – a slinky, sensual theatre dance style that at times will evoke the quality of Bob Fosse, but is mixed much more strongly with the full body movement of more traditional jazz styles. His work highlights sensuality, told in the sloping lines of the shoulders, loose wrists, jutting hips and ribs, and the playing of a slow tense movement dynamic of the arm or leg against a held gaze of the eyes. Images ranging from smoky dance halls to the burlesque hall permeate his work. But these are

repeatedly shattered by insertions of strong dance technique – high *battements*, triple *pirouettes*, pencil turns, back *attitude* turns.

Owens teaches his combinations at break neck speed, tossing off spontaneously invented eight counts after eight counts in rapid-fire succession. Woe to the dancer who picks up slowly, or whose concentration is not fully focused. His aim here is to prepare his dancers for the auditions and rehearsal time periods of Hollywood - where full dances can be taught in one day and stage ready for videotaping the next.

Musicality figures strongly, as his movements not only fit well with or as a complement to the music, but he often stretches a single movement over many counts. To make these movements come alive, the dancer must coordinate them with the dynamic impulse of the music, as well as feel the movement throughout its temporal arc.

The last quality that Owens tries to instill in his students is passion, for his work and for the art. When asked what he hopes to give his students, Owens says "I believe it is the energy and passion that I try to bring each day to my class, plus the way in which I hear and feel the music and the way that feeling inspires the movement. I also continue to make the class challenging for my students."

Michael Owens has brought his passion to his class every day, with over three decades of success to prove his methods. The best in the business cite him as a formative teacher. Here's a short list of Owens dancers over the years - Donna McKechnie of *A Chorus Line*, Denise Faye of multiple Broadway shows and the movie *Chicago* fame, film and TV choreographer Michelle Johnston, Broadway director/choreographer Jerry Mitchell, and notable Broadway dancers Charlotte D'Amboise, Jane Krakowski, Eugene Fleming, Valerie Pettiford, Jane Lanier, and Debbie Roshe.

Spence Ford, a veteran of three Broadway shows and now head of theatre dance at Penn State University honored her studies with Owens when she revealed:

> *I adore Michael Owens! His warm-up challenged me and helped me discover how to truly balance my weight over my feet in a natural, relaxed way, whether trying to maintain a static pose or shifting positions from foot to foot. He always had an energetic attitude in class with a wonderful sense of humor - at times, a devilish teasing attitude! I miss being able to run to NYC and take his classes, now that he is LA rooted. He has inspired me since the beginning of my career. He was my partner in my very first job that I booked out of NYC. It was a dinner theatre production of The Boyfriend in North Carolina. We met. We danced. And I fell in love! (Spence Ford)*

Which brings me to Michael Owens as a performer and choreographer. Although he has had success in both of these, from the start Owens felt that he just became too nervous at auditions to successfully chase a career as a performer, and he did not enjoy the business aspect of choreography to pursue that as a career. Owens is shy, and private to the point that he does not allow anyone to photograph his class in session (which is why this article has no class photos of him teaching). If one wants to know more about his work, the only way is to actually see him in action.

Perhaps it is this reason that more dancers do not know of the work of Michael Owens, or have benefited from his expertise as a teacher. It appears that he will always be a respected dance professional whose reputation spreads through word of mouth, and not from self-promotion. This approach favors his students who continue to be affected by his knowledge in classes that are small enough to guarantee personal attention. It has also allowed him to remain true to his ideals, and to find outlets for his teaching where he can present his approach without the influences of celebrity. But it can be honestly said that Michael Owens is a icon to all who have studied with him - he is a dedicated jazz dance professional, unique in his style and approach, who has made a strong impact on jazz dancers and teachers throughout America and Europe. If you ever have chance to experience his class, don't miss it!

Michael Owens currently teaches at Hama's Dance Center, Studio City, CA; the Performing Arts Academy, Van Nuys, CA: and Santa Monica College, Santa Monica, CA; and in periodic master classes at Steps on Broadway in New York.

34
NEW YORK CITY AND JAZZ DANCE -
A FRAGILE STATE?

by Bob Boross

JazzPulsions – January 2010, Copyright Bob Boross

New York City has a legacy as a haven for jazz. But as most serious jazz dancers know, the health of today's jazz scene is not vibrant. Around the world, jazz continues to splinter, evolve, and even be supplanted as America's folk dance. This trend is noticeable in New York right now.

Over the years many jazz dance companies and choreographers have called New York their home – from Jack Cole and Daniel Nagrin on to the masters Matt Mattox and Luigi, through to the next generation of Fred Benjamin and Lynn Simonson, and now to the latest incarnation with jazz artists like Tracie Stanfield and Ginger Cox. Two established choreographers, Danny Buraczeski and Billy Siegenfeld, have started their companies in New York but moved to other cities that were more hospitable. At this current moment, there are just a handful of NYC based companies who wear the badge of "jazz dance."

For instance, the stalwart Fred Benjamin Dance Company was founded in 1968, but now performs only on rare occasions in special programs produced by Dr. Glory Van Scott. Newer companies that espouse a jazz basis are the Synthesis Dance Project of Tracie Stanfield, LiNK! the Movement founded by Ginger Cox, and the theatre dance based Chase Brock Experience. The Synthesis Dance Project has been the most active, presenting regular seasons at the tiny Hudson Theatre. There are modern dance companies, like Alpha Omega Theatrical Dance Company and Forces of Nature, who will at times use jazz dance vocabulary and themes, but they do not label themselves as a jazz dance company.

When speaking of obstacles that jazz dance faces, the relevance of jazz dance to today's concert going audiences is an ongoing question. American society is changing to reflect the influences of technology and the ever-present mass media, which advances "celebrity" as its tool to draw in the viewer. NYC dance critics are primarily educated in ballet or the "downtown dance" of the postmodern, contemporary dancer. Jazz dance, with its emphasis on feeling and accessibility is often ridiculed for its folk roots. For instance, Roslyn Sulcas of the *New York Times*, in reviewing a 2006 performance by the Fred Benjamin Dance Company, said that Benjamin "creates easy-on-the-eye, old fashioned movement," and that "he may not make the most sophisticated dance in New York..."

Choreographer and teacher Tracie Stanfield has experienced this perception, saying "While speaking with presenters, they seemed to want to put me in either the ballet 'box' or the modern 'box.' In order to get my work produced, I have dropped the word 'jazz' from the company description." The dated stigma that jazz dance is not artistic, or worthy of concert production, has not been shaken. And Ginger Cox mentioned that "Ironically, people don't hire me for the traditional jazz, they hire me for my other styles."

A bright spot in jazz dance performance is the group Jazz Choreography Enterprises, headed by president Marian Hyun. For the last few years this non-profit organization has been producing semi-annual jazz dance showcase concerts at the New Dance Group Arts Center. Now that NDG has closed, their next concert is scheduled for mid November 2009 at Manhattan Movement & Arts Center. Hyun echoed the lament about dance critic's perception of jazz dance, saying "I have the feeling dance critics do not think of jazz as having as much artistic merit as ballet or modern, or even tap dance, but since so little jazz is actually presented and reviewed, its hard to say." When pressed about that lack of fully producing jazz companies, she added, "I think jazz dance companies might have a difficult time finding an audience because of the lack of knowledge about jazz dance and the perception among some that it is hopelessly old fashioned. And in a city like NY, where seeing the newest and most exciting art is a goal of many, jazz doesn't create the kind of interest and excitement that contemporary and hip hop does."

The teaching of jazz dance in NYC has also shown changes in recent years. Whereas traditional jazz classes were immensely popular through the mid 1980s, since then a slow decline has taken place as pioneering teachers have been lost to attrition and newly emerging jazz dance forms have taken root. An example of this is the blend of street dance with jazz led by teacher Frank Hatchett.

Hip hop classes are a large portion of nearly all commercial studios like Broadway Dance Center, and even represented at artistic studios like Peridance and Dance New Amsterdam. Contemporary dance classes are the latest trend in the NYC dance scene, mixing in style with both modern dance and jazz classes. At Broadway Dance Center and STEPS, contemporary jazz dance classes now make up more than one third of all jazz dance classes.

The changing ownership of NYC dance studios was a contributing reason to the decline of jazz dance's visibility. Years ago many jazz dance leaders directed their own NYC studios, leading to a strong presence of individual jazz dance philosophies (similar to what is now seen in France). Matt Mattox and Phil Black, as well as Ronn Forella and Charles Kelley were studio owners or dominant teachers, with full daily teaching schedules. Frank Hatchett was the founding teacher of today's Broadway Dance Center, while Jo Jo Smith preceded him at that Times Square location with Jo Jo's Dance Factory. Lynn Simonson's technique blossomed at her SOHO based DanceSpace. Luigi, although still teaching a daily schedule at Studio Maestro, cut an even more dominant feature when he had his own studio location in Lincoln Center. This establishment of jazz dance beach heads in NYC's past contrasts with today's landscape, where the majority of jazz dance teachers are situated in large, multi-room studios - where jazz dance is not a primary philosophy – teaching a limited schedule of classes per week.

That being said, there still are a substantial number of quality jazz dance teachers working in NYC. Susie Taylor, Joe Lanteri, Patti Wilcox, and Debbie Roshe have large classes at STEPS. Sheila Barker, Tracie Stanfield, Ginger Cox, and Sue Samuels lead jazz dance classes at Broadway Dance Center, along with Celia Marta teaching World Jazz and Slam teaching Contemporary Jazz. Dance New Amsterdam, formerly DanceSpace, is still based in the technique of Lynn Simonson. Although Simonson no longer teaches ongoing technique classes in NYC, a staff of teachers certified in her method, led by Katiti King, teaches what is now listed on their schedule as "contemporary jazz - Simonson technique." Stephen Harding of Manhattan Movement & Arts Center has been teaching in NYC for over twenty years. Sharon Wong directs a strong faculty of jazz teachers at the Alvin Ailey American Dance Center. Luigi and Francis Roach teach the Luigi technique at Studio Maestro. Although NYC jazz dance was dealt a blow when international teacher Michael Owens moved to Los Angeles in the 1990s, his technique lives on in NYC with his former students, now teachers - Debbie Roshe and Deborah Zalkind.

A new national trend, affecting all of jazz dance is the immense popularity of television dance shows like *So You Think You Can Dance*. These shows present a terse, commercial style, heavy on contemporary feel, to the overwhelming majority of teen and young adult dancers across the country. When these dancers bring their notion of jazz dance to their classes in NYC or colleges, the market place responds by giving them just those types of classes. This trend can be fought in colleges, where dance professors have more say over course content. For instance, the leading jazz dance choreographer Danny Buraczeski is now a Professor of Dance at Southern Methodist University in Dallas, Texas. He stated "I am in my fifth year at SMU, and with each subsequent first year class, the influence of dance competitions and *So You Think You Can Dance* has gotten stronger and stronger...It takes longer and longer to get the young dancers into the classic idiom. I am happy to say that they do. Some respond right away, but others don't get it."

In my own teaching in NYC, I have seen jazz dance slip away in popularity. My personal take is that our American society has changed radically since the Internet generation of the 1990s. The twentieth century American society was based on the invention of jazz and its many closely related permutations. But our twenty first century is based on technology, which is not "jazz-friendly." The feel and values of popular music has changed. Contemporary has evolved as the appropriate movement for today's mentality. Young dancers do not "feel" music the same way as "old-school" teachers. As Vicki Sheer, director of the Dance Educators of America wrote to me, "I believe contemporary is growing today because it expresses the mess the world is in today. The music is far from uplifting and this is what they are trying to express in dance." Dancers have shorter attention spans, they tend not commit to the long-term study of particular techniques, and their lives are increasingly transitory.

There are many aspects concerning the state of jazz dance that cannot be discussed in this short article, and I'm sure that there are many hard working professionals in jazz who haven't been mentioned. Jazz is not dead - but it surely isn't as dominant as it once was. It may not even be that jazz has lost popularity due to changing its nature, but rather that there are just more alternative dance forms for young dancers to be involved with. The media has latched onto these new forms, as they are fresh and involve the easily swayed younger dancer.

One thing that is missing, unmistakably, are figureheads for jazz dance who galvanize support and lead the movement. Sharon Wong lamented "something that's homegrown needs to be cultivated - there is a need for activists, conventions, and discussions." Jazz dance in NYC right now is like a boat without a rudder. Without strong leadership very soon, jazz could experience a further erosion of importance. Marian Hyun and the efforts of Jazz Choreography Enterprises are examples of what is needed, but we need even more. At one time, Lynn Simonson and DanceSpace were producing evenings of jazz dance company work. The Fred Benjamin Dance Company was actively presenting choreography. Billy Siegenfeld and Danny Buraczeski were

215

performing, and strong jazz dance work was seen in Broadway shows. But most of these stalwarts are no longer active in NYC, leaving a void that is waiting to be filled. Let's hope that it will not take too long before one or more innovative jazz dance artists are able to place their imprint on the next chapter in jazz dance history, setting the stage for new artistic expression in this uniquely American dance form.

35
THE FAMILY OF JAZZ DANCE

by Bob Boross

Jazz Dance: A History of the Roots and Branches

Editors – Lindsay Guarino and Wendy Oliver.
Gainesville: University Press of Florida 2014.
Reprinted with permission of the University Press of Florida.

Since jazz dance is a shared creation of countless individual contributions, there can be no definitive answer to the question "What is Jazz Dance?" Yes, the initial manifestation of jazz dance was a recognizable product of a particular time and circumstance. But as time passed and circumstances changed, so did jazz dance change as it absorbed new realities. My take on the puzzle of how to define it is that the family of jazz dance exceeds the first original creation, and has taken shape in various configurations, however diluted, of that original jazz purity. To limit jazz dance as one particular thing would preclude the infinite possibilities of what jazz dance can become.

To relate this philosophy to my personal practice, I've been fortunate to experience the original form of jazz dance along with many of the newer forms. I've studied vernacular jazz dance with Pepsi Bethel and also as part of theatre dance classes with Lee Theodore, scatted jazz vocals while hitting jazz accents with Billy Siegenfeld, and mastered the precise body isolation exercises of Matt Mattox. I've "*vopped*" with Frank Hatchett and I've slinked through slithery theatrical jazz dance combos with Michael Owens. I also feel that much of my awareness of jazz rhythm comes from my tap dance teachers – Paul Draper, Bob Audy, and Brenda Bufalino. All of these teachers would in some way describe themselves as "jazz" yet I would only characterize

217

Bethel as being of the pure jazz formation. The work of the others embodied elements of the original form, mixed with varying ratios of ballet, modern, and social dance. The jazz dance gene, however subtle, was and is alive in their work.

This is also how I approach the teaching of jazz dance history at Radford University in my course - *The Changing Nature of American Jazz Dance*. I begin by informing my students of how disparate African and European cultural forces inched slowly towards a common time and space on the American continent, slowly picking up speed on their journeys, until at one certain point they merged, creating jazz dance in its greatest purity. Of course this would be the jazz era of the 1910s - 1930s, when American social jazz dancing was closest to its New Orleans roots. It was the time of the Charleston, Lindy, Snake Hips, and other vernacular jazz dances - an explosion of fresh jazz dance movements danced to jazz music by those people who created them.

But as time passed new realities shattered the older upsurge of jazz dance, resulting in shards of jazz purity being flung far into future times and spaces. The shards carried the power and value of the original form, and became the catalyst in the formation of new jazz dance personas. Potency and purity may have been lost in the process, but these newly emerging personas still carry the genes of the original form of jazz dancing.

So what are these "genes" of jazz dance that continually re-surface? For a detailed investigation I could point you towards the writings of Marshall and Jean Stearns(1), Brenda Dixon Gottschild(2), and Felix Begho(3). For now I'll briefly outline these genes as characteristics of movement, rhythm, and expression. Jazz dance takes formation in some visible percentage of all three.

One a pure movement level, there would be the low, grounded stance of the body, combined with a relaxed muscular feel. The knees are primarily bent, and the body will move in natural way - mostly in a parallel leg position. The impulse for movement often begins in the pelvis, with an initial sharp impulse that releases through the arms and

218

legs in a diminishing flow of energy. This close connection of sharp and smooth gives the body a decisive energy of attack that links to the next coming attack through a rolling wave of movement intent.

Body isolations come into play when the dancer either imitates accents in the music or creates a counter rhythm of sophisticated body hits and stretches. Accents are felt in the shoulders, ribs, hips, head, arms, knees - the entire body can be utilized to reflect rhythmic response.

Jazz music has a uniquely sophisticated use of rhythm, and a jazz dancer should in some way draw from this deep well. This is of prime importance when the music danced to is not jazz. Whether it takes shape in sly syncopations or the play of sharp and soft accents that gently slur the center of a straight beat, the jazz dancer should display a skill in internalizing qualities that are found in jazz rhythms, and making those rhythmic qualities visible in the body.

On the level of personal expression, components can be improvisation and/or emotional connection. Jazz dance can be improvised entirely "on the spot" in a direct and spontaneous relationship of the music and the personal movement choices of the dancer. Or it can result from an emotional connection - how the dancer feels when the music washes over him. When emotions are linked to movement, the dancer projects a body language that can express inner feelings. More so than any other concert dance form, jazz dance involves "feeling" and "being" the dance, as opposed to a detached inhabitation.

To judge a dance as being "jazz" would then require an eye keen enough to decipher these key components of movement and emotion, with the goal of determining the ratio of jazz dance characteristics to non-jazz dance characteristics. Dances high on the scale of jazz dance components, for instance, would be Bob Fosse's *Sing Sing Sing* and Donald McKayle's *District Storyville*. Also, Daniel Nagrin's *Strange Hero* and many sections of Alvin Ailey's *Blues Suite*. Lower on the scale would be Peter Martin's *Jazz* (despite its Wynton Marsalis score), Garth Fagan's

Griot (again with a Marsalis score), and a majority of the so-called "contemporary jazz dances" that appear on the television show *So You Think You Can Dance*. To my eye, the defining characteristics of jazz dance movement are strong and visible in those former dances, but are minimal or even non-existent in the latter.

To restrict the "jazz dance" label only to vernacular examples would be too limiting, as there are many fine examples of dance in later decades that draw from the defining jazz characteristics in strong enough doses to honor and make visible the roots of jazz dance. We pay our respects to the founders of jazz dance when we continue to use their remarkable inventions with reverence. I feel that a dance can be seen as "jazz" as long as the choreographer is knowledgeable of jazz dance history and its defining characteristics, and utilizes those characteristics in a fashion that honors the jazz dance heritage.

Notes

(1)   Stearns, Marshall and Jean. Jazz Dance - *The Story of American Vernacular Dance.*

(2)   Gottschild, Brenda Dixon. *Digging the Africanist Presence in American Performance.* Dance and Other Contexts.

(3)   Begho, Felix O. Black Dance Continuum – *Reflections on the Heritage Connection Between African Dance and Afro-American Jazz Dance*, volume 2.

36
FRANK HATCHETT'S JAZZ DANCE

by Bob Boross

Jazz Dance: A History of the Roots and Branches
Editors – Lindsay Guarino and Wendy Oliver.
Gainesville: University Press of Florida 2014.
Reprinted with permission of the University Press of Florida.

Frank Hatchett - the name instantly refers to what is hot, fresh, and new in the world of jazz dance. As a teacher and choreographer for more than 30 years, Frank Hatchett has been a driving force in taking the latest steps and trends from street and social dance and translating them into a jazz dance style he calls "VOP." From the 1960s twist to 1990s hip-hop, Frank Hatchett has been the conduit from the street to the commercial stage.

The unenlightened dancer or observer may jump to the conclusion that Hatchett spends his time picking up on what street dancers are doing and merely transports their steps to the dance studio. In reality, his style is based in strong concert and ethnic dance techniques. To become proficient in VOP, a dancer must know technique as well as have attitude and flair. As Hatchett said in a recent interview at NY's Broadway Dance Center where he leads three classes daily in his style, "You can be a dancer today by just knowing the latest steps, but to me you can see the difference in a dancer that has a knowledge of the older styles. I think that it just makes a stronger, more secure dancer."(1)

In an effort to shed more light on his thoughts on VOP, jazz dance, and the proper training of a jazz dancer, Frank has written a textbook in conjunction with Nancy Myers Gitlin that reveals the building blocks of his life's work. In *Frank Hatchett's Jazz Dance*, some surprising revelations are offered that may cause novices to rethink their methods of dance training and provide a blueprint for teachers who are trying to give their students the best training possible.(2)

Hatchett began his dance career as a young boy in a local Connecticut dance studio. Realizing the need to learn from the best, he sought out teachers known for their success in creating working dancers, like Philadelphia's Eleanor Harris. Harris assisted the young Hatchett in finding work in Atlantic City and Las Vegas revues. Soon after, though, Hatchett boldly opened his own dance studio in a converted Massachusetts storefront in order to teach, find security, and give back to his community. The rapid success of his studio encouraged him to venture to New York where he studied the meticulous, strength-building technique of modern dance pioneer Katherine Dunham. He advanced his knowledge with classes in African, East Indian, and Caribbean dance. It was only after the young Hatchett had established a strong foundation of dance technique that he branched out to develop a signature style that emanated from his soul. His possession of strong technique channeled the feelings in his heart. Hatchett's VOP attitude then found its NYC home when he first began teaching at Jo Jo's Dance Factory in 1980.(3) It flourished in 1984 when he became a co-owner in a new studio at that very same location – the legendary Broadway Dance Center. So although today's observer sees present-day street dance movements when observing his class, Hatchett's life work springs from a career solidly based on dedication, drive, love for teaching, and a detailed knowledge of classic dance methods.

As a teacher, Hatchett expects his students to have technique - from studies in ballet, modern, jazz, and ethnic dance classes. From there, he works to develop the student's ability to VOP. What is VOP? In *Frank Hatchett's Jazz Dance*, VOP is described as "a unique energy put into dance as well as life, a spirit, an attitude" and as a way to "communicate with an audience, to make the audience feel part of the dance experience."(4) VOP is an individual interpretation of jazz or other rhythmic music that comes from the dancer's soul. This description places VOP in agreement with a defining characteristic of jazz dance, where the dancer is encouraged to react individually to musical influences and elicit movements that either reflect the rhythmic structure of the music or display the dancer's personal reaction to the music. VOP demands a marriage of the movement and the music. Therefore the ability to feel music on a personal and emotional level, as well as being able to display that feeling with clarity, confidence, and energy, is essential to a dancer's skill in VOP.

Hatchett feels that many dancers today have a hard time finding the feeling within music, as musical choices on radio and television are limited. "Nowadays," he says, "dancers' knowledge of music is so shallow." So Frank has incorporated some teaching methods that help the dancer to break free from the chains of rigid technique and tap the wellspring of feeling music from the soul. One method is seen easily in the very name - VOP. VOP is not a real word or definition, and the letters do not stand for anything specific. VOP is a verbal incarnation of a feeling. It sounds like what the feeling feels like. When you've finally found it - you're VOPPING! Hatchett finds that this method of creating sounds, rather than solely relying on musical counting, helps to give the dancer a lead to what the movement feels like. Like a jazz singer scatting a melody, Hatchett fills in the spaces between counts with evocative phrases like "zaa baa aah aah" and "chicka chicka boom boom." As Hatchett stated, "It is the art of being the best of both worlds - it's our obligation to feel the music - to ride the music."

Another method in Hatchett's arsenal is to use present-day movements as an unseen portal to a stronger basis in technique.

> There are a couple of teachers who are phenomenal teachers, who are from the old school, and I see that the kids won't go for those [teachers]. And I see kids standing outside their classes and say 'That's dated.' And I say, 'Yeah, but you know, you never know when that might come up at an audition. That's just going to make you stronger as a dancer.' I use current music and I use current moves - different moves from the street, which I've always done from day one. So they like that. And I use that to get into their heads - then I can get them into a technique class.

And without this secure basis for movement skills, acquired by the dancer in technique classes, the ability to relax and find the groove is hindered. As stated in his textbook, the more a dancer can relax, let go, get down, and feel - the more the dancer can project, give attitude, energize - and VOP. The freedom to feel and interpret is based first on a technical understanding of the movement capabilities of the dancer's body, and secondly on an ability to feel music from deep in the soul, allowing that feeling to color, enhance, and embellish the movements a dancer chooses.

Another bit of advice from Hatchett is that dancers today should seek out a variety of classes and dance styles in order to broaden their outlook and prevent the "shallow" dancer that he sees all too often.

I think that dancers need to balance their schedules - to get into a jazz class that is strong technically but is still jazz. And add a class that is freer, so they can still stay on top of what is going on. Then, to get into a theatre class where a teacher might touch on some of the old choreography from musicals. A class like Phil Black used to do, where Monday might be swing, Tuesday might be Latin, and Wednesday might be something from West Side Story. That makes a dancer well versed.(5)

A final caveat was offered by Hatchett as a reminder that an over emphasis on technique can actually hinder a dancer's ability to feel the music. He warns "But more important is to stay away from a class where they are going to put on jazz music and then they just do ballet. They are really not teaching jazz, because there is no marriage of the movement and music."

It is obvious that Frank Hatchett is more than a street dancer. His movement exceeds street dance and his methods borrow from the roots of jazz dance and concert dance techniques. As a teacher, Hatchett has encouraged thousands of dancers to find the feeling of music that resides in them and create a channel for the expression of that feeling. And as a dancer knowledgeable in the concert dance styles of the past, he has brought the integrity and discipline of those forms to young dancers of today - dancers who otherwise may never have been exposed to the movement of Katherine Dunham, Africa, and the Caribbean. Frank Hatchett is a leader in the fields of dance education, jazz dance, and a true original - the creator of his own signature style of jazz dance known as VOP.

Notes

(1)   Hatchett, Frank. Personal Interview with Bob Boross, 1999, New York City. All remarks made by Hatchett came from this interview unless otherwise noted.

(2)   Frank Hatchett and Nancy Meyers Gitlin. *Frank Hatchett's Jazz Dance* (Champaign, IL: Human Kinetics, 2000).

(3)   Hatchett to Boross. December 21, 2011.

(4)   Hatchett and Gitlin. *Frank Hatchett's Jazz Dance*, 3.

(5)   Phil Black was a noted teacher of jazz and tap dance. His New York City studio was a mecca for Broadway dancers from the early 1970s to 1990. He then taught at Broadway Dance Center from 1990 until his retirement in 2003.

37
THE "FREESTYLE" JAZZ DANCE
OF MATT MATTOX

by Bob Boross

Jazz Dance: A History of the Roots and Branches
Editors – Lindsay Guarino and Wendy Oliver.
Gainesville: University Press of Florida 2014.
Reprinted with permission of the University Press of Florida.

Jazz dance is a collective art form, led by pioneers who have advanced its evolution with their individual formulations. One such leader is the dancer-teacher-choreographer Matt Mattox. A product of the finest concert and commercial dance training of the 1940s/50s, Matt Mattox has advanced his own version of a jazz-imbued dance expression over the course of a stellar sixty-five year career. He has significantly impacted Hollywood dance films, Broadway musicals, European concert dance companies, and the training of generations of concert and commercial dancers.(1)

Mattox's work often utilizes movement qualities from jazz dance and has been performed mostly in the commercial theatre. For these reasons dance historians have placed him within the field of jazz dance. However the influences Mattox draws from are eclectic, and his work surpasses the traditional jazz dance vernacular. In his early career Mattox was a gifted ballet dancer, and was mentored by the illustrious ballet choreographer Eugene Loring.(2) Mattox then served a seven-year apprenticeship with the legendary theatrical jazz dance choreographer Jack Cole as one of Cole's preferred dancers in films and Broadway shows. Mattox is also skilled in tap and other dance forms that appear in musicals of the 1940s and 1950s - Flamenco, East Indian, and Ballroom. When permitted to define his own work, Mattox differentiates his

227

dance vocabulary and artistic approach from vernacular and commercial jazz dance by calling his form of jazz dance expression "freestyle." In his article "In Jazz Dance," published in the *Anthology of American Jazz Dance* in 1975, Mattox states "I have always disliked the work "jazz" in connection with the style of movement with which people seem to associate me. I prefer to think of this particular style of movement as being 'freestyle' movement."(3)

Harold "Matt" Mattox was born in Tulsa, Oklahoma, in 1921, and his family moved to Los Angeles in 1931. There he won tap dance contests and partnered for ballroom dance lessons. At age sixteen Mattox took up ballet, eventually studying with ballet teacher Nico Charisse, who at that time was married to Hollywood dance starlet Cyd Charisse. It was she who encouraged Mattox to audition for film and ballet choreographer Eugene Loring. Mattox passed his audition and the very next day began work as a dancer in the Fred Astaire film *Yolanda and the Thief* (1945)(4).

The initial phase of Mattox's lengthy career was as a featured dancer in Hollywood film musicals, where he partnered Marilyn Monroe, Jane Russell, June Allyson, Mitzi Gaynor, Judy Garland, and Cyd Charisse. He appeared in *Gentlemen Prefer Blondes* (1953), *Till The Clouds Roll By* (1946), *The Bandwagon* (1953), and *Pepé* (1960). Mattox's most visible dance role was as Caleb, the third eldest brother in the monumentally successful *Seven Brides for Seven Brothers* (1954).

Mattox was also equally visible as a dancer on Broadway and in touring shows. It was in 1948 that he first met and was hired by Jack Cole as lead dancer in the Broadway bound musical opera *Magdelena(5)*. He danced also for Cole in 1953's ill-fated *Carnival in Flanders(6)*, where Mattox led a trio of devilish, goateed Cole look-a-likes in the show-stopping dance "Spanish Trio." From 1950-1952 Mattox displayed his classical talents as a featured dancer in tours of *Song of Norway* and *Louisiana Purchase*, partnering ballerinas Alexandra Denisova and Vera Zorina in George Balanchine's choreography.

While amassing this remarkable résumé of dance performances,

Mattox was internalizing the building blocks of his later freestyle dance technique in his associations with Eugene Loring and Jack Cole. Although Mattox routinely credits Jack Cole as his major influence, it is important to note that Loring's teaching and experiments in forming a dance class as early as 1948 (also named freestyle) had a strong effect on Mattox's future jazz dance formulation(7).

The knowledge gained from both Loring and Cole benefited Mattox in 1955 when he left Hollywood for opportunities in New York. Mattox was featured in the Joe Layton choreographed musical *Once Upon a Mattress* (1959), and for Cole he danced in *Ziegfeld Follies* (1956). Mattox's career as a choreographer also took flight; he staged dances for the Broadway

musicals *Say Darling* (1958) and *What Makes Sammy Run* (1964), *Aida* at the Metropolitan Opera (1959), and as resident choreographer of the television show *The Bell Telephone Hour* (1959-68).

However it was Mattox's formation of a movement technique influenced by principles from jazz dance that elevated his impact on theatrical dance to a new level. Mattox began teaching Cole's movement vocabulary in NYC at Showcase Studios in January of 1956 and then at the prestigious June Taylor School of Dance in May of 1956(8). In a phone interview, Taylor said:

> *The classes were jammed, I mean, we'd have to hold people off....Students loved his classes because he was probably one of the few teachers who was so disciplined. He didn't allow you to get away with even an eye movement. If the step called for you to*

use your eyes looking to the right, your eyes moved, nothing else. And the dancers loved, absolutely loved it. And he was a damned good teacher!

Mattox soon opened his own school on 56th Street in NYC, behind the City Center Theater. There he invented a series of technique exercises designed to train a dancer in the qualities and precision of ballet along with the isolation movement characterized by jazz dance. The Mattox technique became quite popular, and also across the country in dance conventions. But by 1966, wishing to concentrate more on concert dance choreography and less on commercial work and running a dance studio, Mattox closed his school and became a freelance teacher. During that time he was also appointed as the first Artistic Director of the New Jersey Ballet(10).

In 1970, Mattox again gambled on his future when he abandoned his NYC career for the promise of higher artistic pursuits in Europe.

Mattox moved to London and re-invented himself as a concert jazz dance artist. Teaching at The Place, Mattox formed a concert jazz dance company called *JazzArt*, which was warmly

Matt Mattox and Gianin Loringett – JazzArt dance company. *La Guerre*. London 1972. Image courtesy of Gianin Loringett.

received by critics in London and Scotland(11). In 1975 Mattox moved his base and company once again, this time to Paris, where he opened a dance studio and catalyzed a new French jazz dance community(12).

In 1981 at age 62, Mattox relinquished control of his company and moved to Perpignan in the south of France. Since that time Mattox has maintained an active teaching and choreography career, with invitations to bring his freestyle technique to the Paris Opera Ballet, London's Millennium Dance 2000, Jacob's Pillow, the American Dance Festival, and the Chicago World Jazz Dance Congresses in 1990 and 1992. He retired from active teaching in 2008 at the age of 88.

Freestyle – Philosophy, Style, Technique

The guiding principle of Mattox's freestyle tradition is that once a dancer desires to express a thought in dance form, the dancer will then draw from his mastery of an eclectic range of dance techniques to formulate the proper method of conveying that expression. The dancer is "free" to express what is in his soul, and also "free" of allegiance to any one particular style of dance. In 1969 Mattox advanced his freestyle philosophy as follows:

The word "free" is used because one is left to choose any kind of move he wishes, whether it is a tilt of the head, a flick of the wrist, a rotation of the pelvis, a Shuffle Off to Buffalo, a contraction of the body, the stance of a bullfighter, or a quick double turn and drop to the floor, or a modern fall to a completely prone position. The word "style" is used because one is left to choose whatever style of movement he wants: East Indian, flamenco, early nineteen hundred contemporary, modern, old time vaudeville, folk dancing, ethnic, or a mixture of all of these.(13)

From this philosophy springs Mattox's movement style and technique – with his class exercises supporting the movement he creates. His movement style reflects the qualities of his varied training, with emphasis on execution that is clean, precise, animated, and alive. His locomotor movements normally are in the plié level of jazz dance, while the look of the feet and arms embody the pointed feet and lengthened feeling of ballet. Meanwhile his body level explores all planes - floor work, relevé, high jumps, and of course, movement across the floor in a jazz plié level. The look of the body in many ways is classical, with rounded arm port de bras, while the lower body moves stealthily in a jazz plié, shifting weight without recognizable effort.

The Mattox class technique is crafted in the progression of a ballet class but is performed standing at center floor. The class design includes exercises for demi-plié, plié, tendu, dégagé, ronde jambe, piqué, and so on. However, these exercises are often performed with a parallel hip alignment, in a plié level, and peppered with body isolations of the head, shoulders, rib cage, and hips. Arm port de bras of a jazz-ballet mixture are integrated with leg exercises, challenging the dancer's mastery of polycentric and polyrhythmic complexity.

The class continues with more strength building in floor work and stretching exercises, followed by standing jumps in a parallel leg position. The culmination of his class is a unique, extended dance combination set to a variety of music styles – swing, pop, densely textured instrumentals, and even new age classical. Each combination demands attention to design, rhythm, attack, nuance, feeling, and drive to achieve perfection in execution. It is here where the fullest example of his freestyle dance expression becomes visible - a personal reaction to the feelings brought on by his choice of music and his thoughts, which takes shape in a movement vocabulary consisting of a unique combination of jazz, ballet, and other mastered dance forms.

CONCLUSION

Matt Mattox often utilizes movement qualities of jazz dance in many of his creations for both the concert stage and the commercial theatre. When asked to define his work, he prefers the label "freestyle" rather than "jazz dance." Yet it is obvious that the field of jazz dance has been significantly influenced by his contributions. Mattox is a revered founding father of European jazz dance, and a historically important jazz dance pioneer in America. As evidenced by his stellar performance career in the commercial theatre, his eclectic choreographic achievements in film, television, theatre and operas, and his unique creation of an internationally prominent, jazz dance inspired style and technique, Matt Mattox clearly stands as a "grandmaster" in the greater field of jazz dance.

Notes

1. This article was written prior to Mattox's death in February 2013.

2. Lucia Chase, Mattox ABT Letter File, Dance Collection, Library of Performing Arts at Lincoln Center, New York. Based solely on ballet choreographer Eugene Loring's glowing recommendation, company director Lucia Chase invited Mattox to join Ballet Theatre in 1948 as a soloist.

3. Matt Mattox, "In Jazz Dance," in *Anthology of American Jazz Dance*, ed. Gus Giordano (Evanston, IL: Orion, 1975), 100-101.

4. Bob Boross, "Image of Perfection: The Freestyle Dance of Matt Mattox" (MA Thesis, Gallatin Division, New York University, 1994), 56.

5. Mattox to Boross, October 18, 1993. Some authors have erroneously reported that Mattox was a member of Cole's 1944-48 Columbia Pictures dance group.

6. *Carnival in Flanders* was panned by New York critics, and it closed after six performances.

7. Eugene Loring (1911-82) was a prominent dancer in ballets by Balanchine, Fokine, and de Mille. In 1947 he founded the American School of Dance in Los Angeles, and within a year he was teaching a hybrid dance technique that he called freestyle.

8. Mattox to Boross, October 18. 1993.

9. June Taylor, interview with Boross, July 27, 1994.

10. Mattox to Boross, September 20, 1994.

11. John Percival, "London Reviews," *Dance and Dancers*, January 1975, 36.

12. Maggie Lewis, "American Jazz Dance- Alive and Well and Living in Paris," *Christian Science Monitor*, December 2, 1980, B18-19.

13. Mattox, "In Jazz Dance," 101.

Printed in Great Britain
by Amazon